CALLED AND CONTRACTED

CALLED AND CONTRACTED

A Faith-Based Organization's Complete Guide to Government Contracts, Grants & Federal Portals

---

PEN 2 PAPER PUBLISHERS

Called and Contracted: A Faith-Based Organization's Complete Guide to Government Contracts, Grants & Federal Portals

Copyright © 2026 Pen 2 Paper Publishers

All rights reserved.

No part of this publication may be reproduced, distributed, or transmitted in any form or by any means, including photocopying, recording, or other electronic or mechanical methods, without the prior written permission of the publisher, except in the case of brief quotations embodied in critical reviews and certain other noncommercial uses permitted by copyright law.

Published by Pen 2 Paper Publishers

For permissions requests and bulk purchasing inquiries, contact the publisher directly.

ISBN: 979-8-9958776-2-2

Printed in the United States of America

First Edition, 2026

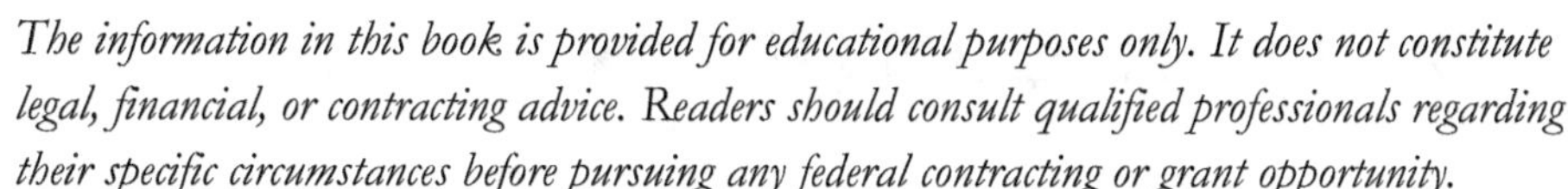
The information in this book is provided for educational purposes only. It does not constitute legal, financial, or contracting advice. Readers should consult qualified professionals regarding their specific circumstances before pursuing any federal contracting or grant opportunity.

To every ministry leader building something that will outlast them —

may these pages open doors, your faith already unlocked.

TABLE OF CONTENTS

INTRODUCTION

Why Faith Organizations Belong in the Federal Marketplace

"Does someone like me belong here?"

The federal government spent nearly $7 trillion last year. A significant portion of that money funds social services, housing, homelessness programs, veterans services, community development, youth programs, and family support. That is the work faith organizations do every day — often with fewer resources, more heart, and deeper community trust than any contractor on the government's preferred vendor list. The question isn't whether your mission qualifies. The question is: why haven't you been funded for it yet?

If you are a faith leader, a nonprofit founder, or a ministry director who has ever wondered whether the federal government's resources have anything to do with you, this book was written to answer that question. And the answer is yes. Unequivocally, historically, and legally: yes.

The Promise — What's Available and Why It Matters

The federal marketplace is not a monolith. It is a vast, multifaceted ecosystem of agencies, programs, contracts, grants, and cooperative agreements — each designed to address a specific public need. And a substantial portion of those programs is designed to fund exactly what faith organizations already do.

Key agencies funding community-facing programs include the Department of Housing and Urban Development, which funds housing stability and homelessness prevention; the Department of Health and Human Services, which funds social services and behavioral health; the Department of Labor, which funds workforce training and veteran employment; the Department of Veterans Affairs, which funds veteran care and reintegration; the U.S. Department of Agriculture, which funds nutrition and rural community programs; FEMA, which funds emergency and disaster relief services; and the Department of Education, which funds youth development and literacy initiatives. That list reads like a summary of what most faith organizations do on a typical Tuesday.

Here is the gap: faith leaders are often the last to know that funding exists for their exact mission. Commercial contractors and professional grant writers have been navigating these portals for decades. Faith organizations, meanwhile, have been funding their work through tithes, offerings, and the occasional local foundation grant — assuming that federal dollars were for someone else. They are not. They never were.

The Myth — Why Faith Leaders Think This Isn't for Them

The most common reason faith leaders stay out of the federal marketplace is a misunderstanding of the law. They believe — reasonably, given how often it's repeated — that the separation of church and state means government and religion cannot mix. It does not mean that.

The First Amendment's Establishment Clause prohibits the government from establishing a national religion or giving preferential treatment to one religion over another. It does not prohibit faith organizations from receiving federal funding to deliver non-religious social services. Courts have consistently upheld the right of faith-based organizations to compete for and receive federal funding, provided that the funded activities are secular in nature and that participation is not conditioned on religious activity.

In plain terms, your feeding program can receive federal funding. Your housing assistance ministry can receive federal funding. Your workforce training program can receive federal funding. What the government cannot fund is the Sunday sermon. Everything else your ministry does that serves the community — everything that addresses a documented social need — is eligible.

The Small Business Administration has gone further, recently moving to remove regulations that had previously restricted faith-based organizations from participating in certain SBA programs. The policy environment is not just permitting faith org participation — it is actively encouraging it.

The Policy Moment — Why Right Now Is the Right Time

Timing matters in the federal marketplace, and this moment is significant. The current federal administration has explicitly identified faith-based organizations as priority government partners. Policy directives from the highest levels of the executive branch have instructed agencies, including the SBA, HUD, HHS, and USAID, to expand their partnerships with faith-based and community organizations.

The Mandate for Leadership — the policy blueprint guiding the current administration's federal priorities — specifically addresses equal treatment for religious entities in government programs. The

SBA's removal of Form 1971, the so-called "Religious Eligibility Worksheet" that had previously screened out certain faith organizations from SBA assistance, is one concrete example of a door that was previously closed being opened.

This is not a permanent condition. Policy environments shift. The organizations that establish their federal presence now — that get registered, get certified, get funded, and build past performance records during this window — will be positioned to sustain that presence regardless of what political winds shift in the years ahead. The time to act is not when the door is wide open. The time to act is when it first begins to open. That moment is now.

What This Book Will Do For You

Called and Contracted is a working guide. It will walk you through the specific, practical steps of entering the federal marketplace as a faith-based organization — from registering on SAM.gov to identifying your NAICS codes and certifications to finding opportunities that match your mission to responding to those opportunities with the confidence of an organization that knows its value.

By the time you finish this book, you will have completed your SAM.gov registration, identified the right codes and certifications for your ministry model, found at least three federal programs relevant to your mission, drafted your capability statement, and submitted or prepared to submit your first federal response. This is not aspirational. These are the outputs of each chapter's Closing Action, and they build on each other from the first page to the last.

More than the mechanics, this book will give you a framework for thinking about the federal marketplace — not as a foreign world you're trying to crack, but as an extension of the mission you've already been living.

How to Use This Book

Read it from front to back the first time. The chapters build on each other intentionally — each one assumes you've absorbed what came before. After your first read, come back to individual chapters as reference guides as needed. Chapter 4 on SAM.gov registration. Chapter 5 on NAICS codes. Chapter 9 on your capability statement. These chapters are written to stand alone as working references.

Most importantly: do the Closing Action at the end of each chapter. This book only works if you work it. Every Closing Action is concrete, achievable, and directly connected to the chapter's promise. None of them will take more than an hour. Together, they will build everything you need to enter the federal marketplace as a prepared, registered, and competitive organization.

Real Talk

You don't have to choose between your calling and your contract. Called and Contracted was written for the faith leader who already knows their mission matters — and is finally ready to make the federal government agree.

Closing Action

Make a decision: this book is not casual reading. It is a working guide. Commit to completing the Closing Action at the end of each chapter. Write that commitment down somewhere you will see it. Sign it if you need to. What you're building is worth the commitment.

Before we talk about portals, contracts, and capability statements, we need to talk about you. The most important thing to understand before you enter the federal marketplace is that you are already qualified.

PART ONE | THE CALLING

CHAPTER ONE

Your Mission IS Your Qualification

"Does my ministry background count for anything here?"

Government agencies have a problem. They are trying to reach communities that have been historically underserved by government systems — and they are hiring contractors to bridge that gap. Meanwhile, faith leaders who have spent decades earning trust in those very communities are sitting outside the door, convinced they don't belong at the table. That is the gap. And you are the answer.

What the Government Is Actually Buying

Here's something that surprises most faith leaders when they first hear it: the federal government is not just buying fighter jets and office supplies. A significant and growing portion of the federal budget funds the same work faith organizations have been doing for generations — social services, housing support, homelessness prevention, veterans reintegration, workforce training, youth development, family counseling, and community nutrition programs.

When a federal agency issues a contract or a grant, it is essentially saying: " We need someone who can deliver these services to this population in this community. Can you do it?" And the evaluation criteria aren't mystical. They're practical. Agencies want to know whether you've done work like this before, whether your team is qualified to deliver it, and whether your organization has the infrastructure to manage the funding responsibly.

In contracting language, that history of delivering services is called "past performance." It is one of the most heavily weighted factors in federal contract evaluation. And here is what every faith leader needs to understand: the programs you have been running — the feeding programs, the counseling ministries, the after-school initiatives, the housing assistance referrals — that is your past performance. You have already been doing the work the government is trying to fund. The only missing piece is the paperwork.

How Ministry Track Record Translates to Past Performance

Past performance is not about who you know or how long you've been in business. It is documented proof that your organization has delivered a service to a population and produced measurable outcomes. When evaluators score a proposal, they look for three things: the scope of the work you've done, the scale at which you delivered it, and the outcomes you achieved.

Your ministry has all three.

Consider how a typical faith-based program reads in the language of federal contracting. A feeding program that serves 500 families every Saturday becomes: "Delivered weekly food security services to 500 low-income households, distributing approximately 2,600 meals per month over a three-year period." A counseling ministry with a caseload of 40 active clients becomes: "Provided behavioral health support and case management services to 40 individuals annually, including referrals to mental health resources, employment services, and emergency housing assistance." A church partnership with the county school system becomes: "Maintained a formalized partnership with the County School District to provide after-school programming for 75 youth ages 10 to 17, with documented improvements in academic attendance and family stability."

None of that language is dishonest. It is a translation. You did the work. Now you are describing it in the language the evaluator needs to read.

The important thing is to start documenting now, even if your first federal opportunity is six months away. Every program you run today is evidence you can use tomorrow. Start keeping records: how many people you served, what services you provided, over what time period, and what changed for them as a result. That file is the beginning of your federal portfolio.

Community Trust as a Competitive Advantage

Federal agencies spend considerable resources trying to reach communities that commercial contractors often struggle to connect with — communities where language barriers, cultural differences, and geographic isolation have made it difficult for traditional service providers to gain a foothold. Faith organizations have been doing this work quietly and effectively for decades.

That is not a soft advantage. It is a documented competitive differentiator.

When a Department of Housing and Urban Development program officer is looking for a partner to run a housing stability initiative in a specific neighborhood, they need someone who can actually get people through the door. Government-issued flyers don't do that.

Contracted call centers don't do that. A faith organization that has been meeting that neighborhood's needs for twenty years — where people know the pastor by name, where the food pantry is a weekly institution, where the building itself is a symbol of safety — that does it.

Your community relationships are an asset. In federal contracting, they appear in your capability statement as your differentiators — the specific qualities that make your organization uniquely suited to deliver a service that other organizations cannot replicate. A prime contractor who has a government relationship but no community presence needs you. That is how teaming arrangements are formed, and how faith organizations begin building federal track records even before winning their first solo contract.

The Mindset Shift — From Asking Permission to Claiming Access

Here is where most faith leaders get stuck: the mental block that says I'm a pastor, not a contractor. I run a ministry, not a business. This world isn't for me.

That block is understandable. The federal contracting world has its own language, its own portals, its own processes, and its own unwritten rules. It can feel like a foreign country. But the feeling is the obstacle — not the reality.

Look at what you actually do. You manage programs with defined deliverables and deadlines. You coordinate volunteers, staff, and partner organizations. You track outcomes and report to your board. You manage an annual budget with multiple funding streams. You navigate competing priorities, community needs, and stakeholder expectations — all at once.

In contracting terms, that makes you a program manager. A community liaison. A financial administrator. A service delivery expert. The federal government funds people to do all of those things. You have been doing them for years — often without adequate resources, often for a fraction of what a commercial contractor would charge for the same work.

The shift isn't about becoming something new. It is about claiming credit for what you already are. You are not entering a foreign world — you are bringing your demonstrated expertise into a new arena and asking the government to fund the mission it already benefits from.

Your Ministry Credentials in Contracting Language

The translation from ministry language to contracting language is not complicated — it is just a new vocabulary for familiar concepts. Here is the key reference you'll return to throughout this book:

Ministry Language	Federal Contracting Language
Ministry	Program Management
Congregation/community reached	Beneficiaries served / community impact
Church partnerships	Teaming arrangements
Annual budget managed	Financial administration experience
Outreach programs	Community engagement and service delivery

Ministry Language	Federal Contracting Language
Weekly participants	Unduplicated client count
Mission statement	Statement of Work alignment
Board oversight	Organizational governance

The more fluently you speak both languages, the more effectively you'll present your organization in federal applications. The chapters ahead will give you ample practice. For now, the most important thing to understand is that the vocabulary is the only barrier. Everything beneath it — the mission, the track record, the community relationships, the organizational capacity — is already there.

Real Talk
The government doesn't care that you preach on Sundays. It cares that you can deliver results on Monday. Your ministry has been delivering results for years. Now it's time to get funded for it.

Pro Tip
Start a 'Past Performance' folder right now. Every program you've run, every outcome you've documented, every partnership you've maintained — that's your portfolio. We'll

build your capability statement from it in Chapter 9. Don't wait until you need it to start collecting it.

Closing Action

Write your ministry's top 3 program outcomes in one sentence each. Use this format: '[Organization] delivered [service] to [number] [population] in [timeframe], resulting in [outcome].' These three sentences are the foundation of your capability statement — and the beginning of your federal portfolio.

Now that you know your credentials are real, the next question is: what exactly are you applying for? Because "government funding" is not one thing, knowing the difference between a grant, a contract, and a cooperative agreement will determine your entire strategy. Chapter 2 explains each one in plain language, so you can stop guessing and start pursuing the right opportunities for your mission.

— End of Chapter 1 —

PART ONE | THE CALLING

CHAPTER TWO

Grants vs. Contracts vs. Cooperative Agreements

"What even is government money — grants, contracts, what?"

Diana walked out of a federal contracting conference more confused than when she walked in. Three speakers used three different terms — grant, contract, cooperative agreement — as if they were interchangeable. They are not. And not knowing the difference could mean Diana spends six months pursuing the wrong type of funding for her organization. This chapter fixes that in one reading.

Grants — What They Are, Who Issues Them, What They Fund

A grant is federal money given to an organization to carry out a specific activity that benefits the public. Unlike a contract, the government gets no direct product or service in return — it is investing in the work your organization will do on behalf of the communities it serves.

Grants are competitive. Organizations submit proposals, agencies select winners based on published criteria, and the funded organizations carry out the work according to an approved plan. The government doesn't tell you exactly how to do it — that's why grants tend to preserve more organizational autonomy than contracts.

Most federal grant opportunities are posted on Grants.gov, which functions as the single clearinghouse for competitive federal grants. The agencies issuing grants most relevant to faith-based organizations include HUD for housing and community development programs, HHS for social services and behavioral health, DOL for workforce development, the Department of Education for youth and literacy programs, and FEMA for emergency and disaster relief services.

Grants are generally the best fit for nonprofit organizations delivering community services, housing programs, social services, and education initiatives. If your ministry's work falls into any of those categories — and most do — grants are the starting point for your federal funding strategy.

Contracts — What They Are, Who Issues Them, What They Fund

A contract is a binding agreement in which the government pays an organization to deliver a specific product or service. Where a grant funds a program you design, a contract pays you to deliver a scope of work the government defines. Contracts are more structured than grants — they come with specific deliverables, timelines, performance standards, and accountability mechanisms.

Contract opportunities are posted on SAM.gov, and every federal agency issues them — from the Department of Defense to the Department of Veterans Affairs to HHS to GSA. The federal government's contracting budget dwarfs its grant budget, so as your organization matures, contracts represent the larger long-term opportunity.

Contracts are the best fit for organizations that can define and consistently deliver a specific scope of work. If your ministry provides counseling services, workforce training, housing navigation, or veteran support on a regular, documented schedule — you may be closer to contract-ready than you think. The key is being able to describe what you deliver, to whom, in what timeframe, and with what measurable results.

Cooperative Agreements — The Middle Ground

A cooperative agreement is a hybrid of the three. Like a grant, the government provides funding for you to carry out a program. But unlike a grant, the agency plays an active role in the work itself — reviewing progress, providing technical assistance, and collaborating on decisions as the program unfolds. The government is not just a funder; it is a partner.

Cooperative agreements are common in research, pilot programs, and community demonstration projects where the agency wants to learn from the work as it happens. They often appear on Grants.gov alongside traditional grants but operate more like a structured partnership than a straight funding relationship.

Cooperative agreements are best suited for organizations willing to work closely with an agency partner — sharing data, attending regular check-ins, and operating within a more collaborative framework. If your ministry is piloting an innovative model to address homelessness, veterans' reintegration, or economic mobility, a cooperative agreement may be the vehicle to fund and document it at scale.

Which One Is Right for Your Ministry Model

The quickest way to figure out which funding type fits your organization is to ask one question: Does the government want a product or service from us, or does it want us to run a program?

If the government wants a defined product or service — counseling sessions, training hours, housing placements, meals served — that points toward a contract. If the government wants to fund you to run a program with organizational autonomy, that points toward a grant. If the government wants to co-develop and monitor the work alongside you, that points toward a cooperative agreement.

Most faith organizations will start with grants and cooperative agreements before moving into contracts. Grants are more accessible early on — the eligibility requirements tend to be broader, the proposal process is more narrative-driven (which plays to your strengths), and the evaluation criteria often weigh mission alignment and community relationships heavily.

Contracts come later, once you have documented past performance and a clearer sense of what your organization can reliably deliver at scale. The good news is that nothing stops you from pursuing both simultaneously. A healthy federal funding pipeline for a faith-based organization will eventually include all three types. The strategy is knowing where to start.

Where Each Type Appears — Your Portal Map

Knowing what type of funding you're pursuing tells you exactly where to look for it. Here is the map you will use throughout this book:

Funding Type	Where to Find It	Best Fit For
Grant	Grants.gov	Nonprofits delivering community programs with organizational autonomy
Contract	SAM.gov	Orgs that can define and deliver a specific, repeatable scope of work
Cooperative Agreement	Grants.gov	Orgs piloting innovative models with active agency partnership

There is one additional portal worth knowing: USASpending.gov. This is not where you apply for anything — it is a research tool that shows you who is already receiving federal funding and for what. Before you pursue any opportunity, USASpending.gov tells you which agencies are already investing in your mission area, which organizations are already winning, and what the funding landscape looks like in your region. Chapter 7 covers all three portals in depth. For now, bookmark all three: grants.gov, sam.gov, and usaspending.gov.

Definition

Assistance Listing Number (ALN): Every federal assistance program has a unique identifying number — formerly called the CFDA number. When you find a grant program that matches your mission, record its ALN. It is your shortcut to finding that program's current and past opportunities on

Grants.gov and to locating organizations already funded under that same program on USASpending.gov.

Watch Out

Do not confuse a Sources Sought notice with a contract offer. A Sources Sought is market research — the agency is asking 'who's out there?' before writing the actual solicitation. Responding to a Sources Sought does not obligate you to bid, and bidding does not guarantee you'll win—more on this in Chapter 10.

Closing Action

Review your current ministry programs and assign each one a funding-type label: Grant, Contract, or Cooperative Agreement. Use the question 'Does the government want a service from us, or does it want us to run a program?' to guide your answer. This list is the first draft of your federal funding strategy.

Now you know what you're going after. The next question is: are you ready to go get it? Before you log in to any portal or submit any application, certain foundational elements must be in place. Chapter 3 walks you through exactly what those are — and how to confirm you have everything before you take your first step.

— End of Chapter 2 —

PART ONE | THE CALLING

CHAPTER THREE

Getting Your House in Order: Legal Structure, EIN & Entity Readiness

"What do I need to have in place before I start?"

The good news: most faith organizations already have more of the foundational pieces in place than they realize. The challenging news: missing pieces can stop your entire registration process cold. SAM.gov will ask for specific information at specific steps — and if you don't have it on hand, you'll either enter incorrect data or abandon the process mid-registration. Neither outcome serves you. This chapter is your preflight checklist. Run through it once, confirm what you have, address what you don't, and you'll walk into SAM.gov ready to register without stopping.

Legal Entity Structure — What You Need to Be

The federal government registers entities — legal organizations with a formal structure recognized by the state and the IRS. Before you register on SAM.gov, your organization must be a legal entity. That sounds more complicated than it is, because most ministries and faith-based nonprofits are already structured correctly.

If your organization is a 501(c)(3) nonprofit, you are already a legal entity. Your IRS determination letter is the documentation that proves it. That letter is one of the most important documents in your federal contracting folder, and you should have a scanned copy accessible at all times. Your 501(c)(3) status does more than confirm your legal structure — it opens grant eligibility that is unavailable to for-profit businesses and positions you as a community-benefit organization in the eyes of federal program officers.

If your organization is structured as an LLC or a corporation — whether you are operating a faith-adjacent business rather than a traditional nonprofit — you are still fully eligible. LLCs and corporations are valid legal entities for SAM.gov registration. Your NAICS codes and certifications will position you as a faith-based community service provider, regardless of your entity type.

If you haven't yet filed for 501(c)(3) status and your ministry primarily delivers social services, housing support, or community programs, it is worth discussing with a nonprofit attorney or accountant. The application process (IRS Form 1023 or the simplified 1023-EZ for smaller organizations) takes time. Still, the benefits — including grant eligibility and donor tax deductibility — make it worth the investment for most faith-based organizations whose primary funding will come from federal grants.

Your EIN — What It Is and Where It Lives

Your EIN — Employer Identification Number — is your organization's federal tax identification number, assigned by the IRS. Think of it as a Social Security number for your entity. Every registered business and nonprofit in the United States has one, and you cannot complete a SAM.gov registration without it.

If your organization already has an EIN, it appears on your prior tax filings (Form 990 for nonprofits, Form 1120 for corporations), on your original IRS EIN confirmation letter, and on any bank account documents opened in the organization's name. If you can't locate it, call the IRS Business & Specialty Tax Line at 800-829-4933. They can verify your EIN over the phone.

If your organization doesn't yet have an EIN, the application is free and takes minutes at IRS.gov. You'll receive your EIN immediately upon completing the online application during IRS business hours. Do not pay any third-party service to apply for your EIN — the IRS charges nothing for this.

One critical note: SAM.gov validates your EIN directly with the IRS during registration. This means the legal name on your SAM.gov registration must match exactly what appears in the IRS system — word for word, including any punctuation. A mismatch between your SAM.gov entity name and your IRS name is one of the most common causes of registration failures. Pull out your EIN confirmation letter before you begin, and use the name exactly as it appears there.

Your UEI — The Federal Identifier That Replaces DUNS

If you've heard of a DUNS number — the nine-digit Dun & Bradstreet identifier that federal contractors used for decades — you can set that aside. In April 2022, the federal government transitioned to the Unique Entity Identifier, or UEI, as the standard identifier for all entities in the federal system.

Here's the important distinction: you don't apply for a UEI separately. Your UEI is assigned automatically when you register on SAM.gov. If you have never registered on SAM.gov before, you will receive your UEI at the beginning of the registration process and carry it for the life of your organization's federal identity. If you registered on SAM.gov before the 2022 transition, your existing registration already has a UEI in your account dashboard.

Once assigned, your UEI stays with your organization regardless of whether your SAM.gov registration lapses or expires. Record it in your Federal Contracting Documents folder the moment it appears. You will use it on every federal form, every capability statement, every Sources Sought response, and every proposal you submit for the rest of your organization's federal contracting life.

CAGE Code — What It Is and When You Need It

The CAGE Code — Commercial and Government Entity Code — is a five-character alphanumeric identifier assigned by the Defense Logistics Agency after your SAM.gov registration becomes active. Like the UEI, you do not apply for it separately. It is assigned automatically once the government processes your registration.

Your CAGE Code is required for Department of Defense contracts and appears on many federal forms alongside your UEI. Not every opportunity will require a CAGE Code — grant applications generally don't — but once you begin pursuing contracts, it becomes a standard piece of your organizational identity in the federal system. Record it alongside your UEI the moment it appears in your SAM.gov profile.

Business Bank Account — The Final Piece Before You Register

Federal payments are processed through Electronic Funds Transfer, which means the government deposits awards directly into a US bank account. That account must be held in the legal name of the registered entity — not a personal account, not a joint account, not an account under a ministry leader's personal name.

This is a requirement, not a preference. If your entity name on SAM.gov and your bank account name don't match, your payment can be rejected or flagged by the Treasury. Before you begin registration, confirm that you have a dedicated business checking account in the exact legal name of your organization. If you don't, open one. Most banks will open a business account with your EIN and state formation documents. This step takes a few days and is worth completing well before you sit down to register.

During SAM.gov registration, you will enter your bank's nine-digit routing number and your account number. Have both on hand. If you enter them incorrectly and an award payment is made to the wrong account, the correction process is time-consuming. Double-check before you submit.

State Registration and Physical Address

Your organization must be registered in the state where it operates. For nonprofits, your 501(c)(3) filing with the IRS typically satisfies state requirements in many states, but some states require a separate state-level charitable registration or business filing. Confirm your state registration is current before you begin SAM.gov registration.

You will also need a physical mailing address for your organization — a P.O. Box is generally not acceptable as a primary address in SAM.gov. If your ministry operates out of a church building, a community center, or a leased office, use that address. The address on your SAM.gov registration should match the address on your IRS filings and state registration documents as closely as possible.

Your Pre-Registration Checklist

Work through this checklist before you open SAM.gov. Every item on it will be required at some point in the registration process. Having them all confirmed in advance means your registration proceeds in a single uninterrupted session rather than starting and stopping.

Done	Item
☐	Legal entity formed and registered in your state (LLC, corporation, or nonprofit)
☐	501(c)(3) IRS determination letter located and scanned (nonprofits)
☐	EIN confirmed — legal name matches IRS records exactly
☐	Business bank account open and in the entity's legal name
☐	Bank routing number and account number on hand
☐	Physical mailing address confirmed (not a P.O. Box)
☐	State registration is current and in good standing
☐	NAICS codes identified (covered in Chapter 5 — note them here before registration)

Pro Tip

Take a photo of your EIN confirmation letter and save it in a dedicated folder labeled 'Federal Contracting Documents.' You will reference your EIN more times than you can count. That same folder should eventually hold your UEI, CAGE Code, SAM.gov login credentials, registration expiration date, and copies of all active certifications.

Watch Out

Do not use a personal bank account for federal payments — even temporarily. If your entity name and bank account name don't match, your payment can be rejected or flagged. Open the business account before you register, not after you win.

Closing Action

Work through the Pre-Registration Checklist above. Check off what you have. For each missing item, write one action step and a target completion date. Your SAM.gov registration date is the deadline for all eight items. Do not begin registration until every box is checked.

Your house is in order. Your keys are ready. Now it's time to walk through the front door. Chapter 4 takes you through the SAM.gov registration process step by step, with specific guidance for nonprofit entities and faith-based organizations — so you know exactly what each screen is asking and exactly what to enter.

— End of Chapter 3 —

PART TWO | THE CONTRACT

CHAPTER FOUR

Creating Your SAM.gov Account as a Nonprofit or Faith Organization

"How do I actually get on SAM.gov?"

SAM.gov — the System for Award Management — is the front door to the entire federal marketplace. Every organization that wants to receive a federal contract or grant must be registered and active on SAM.gov. No exceptions. Without it, a contracting officer cannot legally pay you, a grant officer cannot process your award, and your organization is invisible to every procurement system in the federal government.

The good news is that registration is free, it's done entirely online, and once you understand what each section is asking, it's navigable. The less good news is that it's a government website, which means it was designed by committees, for audiences far broader than you, and it shows. This chapter translates every step into plain language so you know exactly what you're clicking, exactly what you're entering, and exactly what to do when something doesn't look right.

Before You Log In — What to Have Ready

The single biggest mistake people make when registering on SAM.gov is starting without everything they need. The registration process has multiple sections, and if you don't have a required piece of information on hand, you'll either enter something incorrectly or abandon the session — which means starting over.

Before you open sam.gov, have the following items physically in front of you or pulled up on a second screen: your EIN and the exact legal name as it appears in your IRS records, your organization's physical address, your bank's routing number and your account number, the NAICS codes you identified for your organization (from Chapter 5 — if you haven't done that yet, do it before registration), and your organization's fiscal year end date. If you have a 501(c)(3) determination letter, have it available as well. Ten minutes of preparation here saves an hour of frustration later.

Step One — Create Your Login.gov Account

SAM.gov uses Login.gov for identity verification. Before you can access SAM.gov, you need a Login.gov account. If you already have one — because you've used it for another federal system — you can skip this step. If you don't, here's how to set it up.

Go to login.gov and select Create an account. You'll enter an email address and create a strong password. Login.gov will then ask you to set up a second authentication method — this is the step that trips people up. You have several options: a phone number that can receive a text message, an authentication app, a security key, or backup codes. For most users, the text message option is the simplest. Choose your method, verify it, and your Login.gov account is active.

One important decision: use your organization's official email address, not a personal one. SAM.gov sends registration confirmations, renewal reminders, and opportunity notifications to the email on file. If that email is a personal account that you check inconsistently, you will miss time-sensitive notifications. Use an email address your organization monitors regularly.

Step Two — The Registration Process, Section by Section

Once you're logged into SAM.gov through Login.gov, select Get Started and then Register Your Entity. The registration is organized into sections that build on each other. Here is what each section asks and what you need to enter:

Step	Section	What to Enter
1	**Entity Type**	Select Nonprofit Organization if you are a 501(c)(3). Select Business or Organization if you are an LLC or corporation.
2	**Core Data**	Enter your EIN exactly as it appears in IRS records. SAM.gov will validate this in real time. If it fails, your entity name or EIN is mismatched — correct the discrepancy before proceeding.
3	**Legal Business Name**	Must match your IRS records word for word. Include any articles (The, A), abbreviations, and punctuation exactly as filed.

Step	Section	What to Enter
4	**Physical Address**	Use your official organizational address — not a P.O. Box. Must match your state registration records.
5	**Goods & Services**	Enter your NAICS codes here. Your primary code first, then secondary codes. You can return to update these later.
6	**Financial Information**	Enter your bank routing number and account number for Electronic Funds Transfer (EFT). Double-check both before submitting.
7	**Points of Contact**	Enter the name, title, phone, and email of the person responsible for the registration. This is the individual SAM.gov and agency officers will contact.
8	**Financial Assistance**	Complete this section fully if you are seeking grants. For nonprofits, this section determines grant eligibility. Do not skip or rush it.
9	**Review & Submit**	Review every section before submitting. Errors here are correctable, but they delay your activation. Processing takes 7–10 business days after submission.

Key Differences for Nonprofits and Faith Organizations

The SAM.gov registration process is the same for all entity types, but there are a few places where nonprofit and faith-based organizations need to pay specific attention.

Entity type selection matters. When SAM.gov asks you to identify your entity type, nonprofits should select Nonprofit Organization — not Business or Organization. This distinction affects which assistance programs you are eligible for and how your organization appears in agency searches. Faith-based organizations that operate as for-profit businesses (LLCs, S-Corps) should select the appropriate business type and rely on their NAICS codes and certifications to signal their identity as faith-based community service organizations.

The Financial Assistance section is critical for grant seekers. This section of registration determines your eligibility for federal assistance programs — meaning grants and cooperative agreements. For nonprofits, it asks about your fiscal year, your auditing practices, and your organizational structure. Complete every field carefully and accurately. Incomplete Financial Assistance sections are one of the most common reasons nonprofits find themselves ineligible for grant programs they should qualify for.

Your 501(c)(3) status should be clearly reflected in your registration. When the system asks about tax-exempt status, confirm it and enter your IRS determination date. This information appears in your public SAM.gov profile and signals to grant officers that your organization is a community-benefit nonprofit.

Understanding Your Registration Status

After you submit your registration, SAM.gov moves it through a validation process. Understanding the status labels prevents unnecessary anxiety during the wait.

Submitted means your registration has been received and is in the processing queue. This is not the same as active — you cannot receive federal awards at this stage. Processing typically takes 7 to 10 business days, though it can occasionally take longer during high-volume periods.

Active means your registration has been fully processed and validated. You are in the federal system. Contracting officers can find you, agencies can award to you, and you can receive federal payments. This is the status you are working toward.

Inactive or Expired means your registration has lapsed — either it was never completed or it was not renewed before the expiration date. An inactive registration disqualifies your organization from receiving new awards and can affect payment on existing awards. Check your status regularly in your SAM.gov dashboard, and never allow your registration to lapse.

Annual Renewal — The Rule You Cannot Forget

Your SAM.gov registration expires exactly 12 months from the date it became active. It does not auto-renew. There is no grace period. If your registration expires, you lose eligibility for new awards immediately, and agencies processing existing awards may place payments on hold until the registration is restored.

The renewal process is identical to the original registration — you log in, verify and update your information, and resubmit. Processing takes the same 7 to 10 business days. This means you should begin your renewal no later than 30 days before your expiration date, and ideally 60 days out. Set a recurring calendar reminder on the day your registration goes active. Do not leave this to memory.

Your expiration date appears in your SAM.gov entity dashboard. Record it in your Federal Contracting Documents folder alongside your UEI and CAGE Code. Treat it as a non-negotiable organizational deadline — because it is.

Step-by-Step

Before you begin registration: gather your EIN and IRS legal name, your organization's physical address, your bank routing number and account number, your NAICS codes, your fiscal year-end date, and your 501(c)(3) determination letter (if applicable). Open a second browser window with these items pulled up before you start filling out the SAM.gov form.

Watch Out

SAM.gov fraud is real and increasing. If you receive an email, phone call, or letter asking you to pay to register or renew on SAM.gov, it is a scam. The federal government does not charge for SAM.gov registration. Go directly to sam.gov and do not click links in unsolicited emails claiming to be from SAM.gov, GSA, or any federal agency.

Closing Action

Begin your SAM.gov registration today — or log in to verify your existing registration is active. Record your UEI, your registration expiration date, and your CAGE Code (once assigned) in your Federal Contracting Documents folder. Set a calendar reminder 60 days before your expiration date. Do not close this chapter without completing at least one of these three actions.

You are registered — or ready to register. But one of the most important decisions you'll make during registration is which NAICS codes you select. Get them right, and the right opportunities will find you. Get them wrong, and you'll spend hours searching for opportunities that should have come to you automatically. Chapter 5 shows you exactly which codes match your ministry model and how to use them strategically.

— End of Chapter 4 —

PART TWO | THE CONTRACT

CHAPTER FIVE

Choosing the Right NAICS Codes for Ministry-Based Services

"Which codes actually describe what I do?"

Your NAICS code is how the federal government categorizes your organization's activities. Contracting officers use NAICS codes to search for qualified vendors. Grant programs are structured around them. They filter set-aside opportunities. When a procurement official logs in to SAM.gov to find organizations that provide youth services, housing support, or veteran reintegration programs, the NAICS code is the first filter they apply. If yours are wrong — or if you're only using one when you should be using five — you become invisible to the very opportunities your ministry was built to pursue. This chapter makes sure that doesn't happen.

What NAICS Codes Are and Why They Matter

NAICS stands for North American Industry Classification System. It is a standardized classification system used by the US, Canada, and Mexico to categorize economic activity. Every business and nonprofit in the federal system is assigned at least one six-digit NAICS code, and that code determines which categories of federal opportunities you appear in when agencies search for vendors.

NAICS codes matter for three reasons beyond simple categorization. First, they determine your small business size standard — the revenue or employee threshold below which the SBA classifies you as a small business, making you eligible for small business set-aside contracts. Different NAICS codes have different size standards, so the codes you select affect which set-aside opportunities you qualify for. Second, they signal your capabilities to contracting officers seeking specific expertise. Third, they connect you to the specific solicitations and grant programs that are written around those codes — opportunities that may never appear in a general keyword search but surface automatically when you're properly coded.

You can list multiple NAICS codes in SAM.gov. There is no requirement to limit yourself to one. Most faith-based organizations serving multiple populations should use between three and eight codes, each representing a distinct program area or service type. Selecting too few codes is one of the most common — and most costly — mistakes organizations make when registering.

NAICS Codes Most Relevant to Faith-Based Organizations

The codes below represent the most commonly applicable NAICS categories for faith-based nonprofits and ministry-adjacent organizations. Review each one against your actual programs. If your organization delivers any version of that service — even informally — add the code. You are not limited to codes that perfectly describe your work; you are looking for codes that accurately represent the type of service you provide.

Code	Category	Best Fit For
624110	**Child and Youth Services**	After-school programs, youth development, mentoring, and childcare ministries
624120	**Services for the Elderly and Persons with Disabilities**	Senior ministry, disability support, adult day programs
624190	**Other Individual and Family Services**	General counseling, life skills, emergency assistance, crisis support
624210	**Community Food Services**	Food pantries, feeding programs, nutrition assistance, and community kitchens
624230	**Emergency and Other Relief Services**	Disaster response, emergency housing, crisis intervention
624310	**Vocational Rehabilitation Services**	Workforce training, job readiness, and transitional employment programs
813110	**Religious Organizations**	Primary classification for faith-based orgs — include this always
813319	**Other Social Advocacy Organizations**	Community advocacy, social justice, civic engagement

Code	Category	Best Fit For
611630	**Language Schools**	ESL, literacy programs, immigrant-serving language ministries
611710	**Educational Support Services**	Tutoring, test prep, academic coaching, educational nonprofits
621420	**Outpatient Mental Health and Substance Abuse Centers**	Faith-based counseling centers with licensed staff
623990	**Other Residential Care Facilities**	Transitional housing, recovery homes, faith-based residential programs

How to Search and Confirm Your Codes

The NAICS table above is a starting point, not a complete list. To confirm that you have the right codes for your specific programs, use these three resources together.

The NAICS Association search tool at naics.com allows you to search by keyword and find the codes associated with specific activities. Type in words that describe your programs — 'food assistance,' 'youth mentoring,' 'housing navigation,' 'veteran employment' — and review the results. Read the official code definitions carefully, not just the titles. The definition tells you which activities are included and which are excluded, preventing you from selecting a code that sounds right but technically doesn't apply.

The Census Bureau's official NAICS manual at census.gov/naics is the authoritative source. When in doubt about whether a code applies to your work, look it up here. The definitions are more detailed than the summary descriptions, and they include examples of the types of activities that qualify.

USASpending.gov is your competitive intelligence tool. Search for nonprofit organizations similar to yours that are already receiving federal funding in your city or state. Look at the NAICS codes listed on their award records. This tells you not just what codes exist, but which ones are actively being used to fund work like yours — which is a stronger signal than any description on paper.

Primary vs. Secondary Codes — Using All of Them Strategically

Your primary NAICS code should describe your single most common service — the thing your organization does more than anything else. If you run a feeding program, your primary code is likely 624210. If counseling is your core service, it's 624190. If youth development is your primary work, it's 624110. Choose the code that most accurately represents the majority of your organizational activity.

Secondary codes are where most organizations leave opportunities on the table. Every additional NAICS code you list in SAM.gov is another category of federal opportunities that surfaces when agencies search for vendors with your capabilities. If you run a food pantry and a youth after-school program and a workforce training initiative, you should be coding for all three — not just the primary one.

You can list up to 150 NAICS codes on SAM.gov, though in practice most organizations use between 4 and 12. The goal is not to list every possible code — it is to list every code that accurately reflects a real program or service your organization provides. Each code should be defensible: if a contracting officer calls and asks whether you provide that service, the answer should be an honest yes.

The Code That Belongs on Every Faith Organization's Profile

813110 — Religious Organizations — is your identity code, and it belongs in your SAM.gov profile regardless of what other codes you use. Including it signals that your organization operates from a faith-based framework, which is increasingly relevant as federal agencies expand their partnerships with faith-based and community organizations under current policy directives.

That said, 813110 alone will not surface your organization in most program-specific searches. Contracting officers searching for youth development providers, housing navigators, or workforce training organizations search by the service codes — 624110, 623990, 624310 — not by the organizational identity code. Think of 813110 as the code that identifies you to agencies, while the service codes indicate what you do. Both matters. Neither replaces the other.

How to Add or Update Your Codes in SAM.gov

If you've already registered on SAM.gov and need to add or update your NAICS codes, the process is straightforward. Log in at sam.gov using your Login.gov credentials, navigate to your entity, and select Edit Registration. From there, go to the Goods and Services section where your NAICS codes are stored.

Add your primary code first if it isn't already listed, then add secondary codes one at a time. After making changes, submit your registration for reprocessing — updates to an active registration do not reset your expiration date. Still, they do require a brief reprocessing period, typically two to three business days. Plan your updates well in advance of any opportunities you intend to pursue.

Make it a practice to review your NAICS codes annually when you renew your SAM.gov registration. As your programs grow, your codes should grow with them. A ministry that started with a feeding program and has since added transitional housing and workforce training should be coded for all three — not just the original program that prompted the first registration.

Pro Tip

Before finalizing your NAICS codes, spend 15 minutes on USASpending.gov. Search for two or three faith-based or community nonprofit organizations similar to yours that are already receiving federal funding in your area. Look at the NAICS codes listed on their award records. You're borrowing strategy from organizations that are already winning — and confirming that the codes you've selected are the ones federal agencies actually use to fund work like yours.

Real Talk

813110 is your identity code — include it. But don't stop there. The contracts and grants that fund your programs are filed under the service codes: 624xx, 611xx, 623xx. Think like the contracting officer searching for a vendor, not like the pastor describing your church. Your NAICS codes are a search tool, not a mission statement.

Closing Action

Select your primary NAICS code and at least two secondary codes. Write them down with a one-sentence explanation of why each one fits your organization's actual programs. Then log into SAM.gov and confirm they are listed in your Goods and Services section. If they're not there, add them before you close the browser.

Your NAICS codes tell the government what you do. Certifications tell the government who you are — and why they should prioritize working with you. Some of the most powerful advantages in federal contracting are locked behind certifications that faith-based organizations often don't realize they qualify for. Chapter 6 covers every certification relevant to your situation and provides a clear next step for each.

— End of Chapter 5 —

PART TWO | THE CONTRACT

CHAPTER SIX

Certifications That Give You an Edge

"Does my faith organization qualify for certifications?"

Diana had been in ministry for over two decades. She had led a team, managed a budget, raised funds, and delivered services in communities where very few outside organizations dared to go. But when she logged into the federal marketplace for the first time and saw boxes asking about her certification status — WOSB, EDWOSB, HUBZone, VOSB — she stopped cold. She had never heard any of these terms. She assumed they didn't apply to her. She left the boxes unchecked and moved on.

That was a missed opportunity — and it's one of the most common ones faith-based leaders make when entering the federal marketplace. Certifications are not bureaucratic checkboxes for large corporations. Several of the most powerful ones were designed for exactly the kind of organization Diana leads: community-embedded, mission-driven, often woman-led, often located in economically underserved areas, sometimes connected to military communities. This chapter introduces each one, explains who qualifies, and tells you where to go next.

Why Certifications Matter in the Federal Marketplace

Federal law requires agencies to set aside a portion of their contracting dollars for businesses and organizations that meet certain criteria — women-owned, economically disadvantaged, located in underutilized areas, veteran-operated. These set-asides are not charity. They exist because Congress determined that competition for federal dollars should reflect the full diversity of the American economy, including organizations that serve communities historically left out of major federal investment.

When you hold a valid certification, you become eligible for contracts and grants that are specifically set aside for organizations with that designation. A contracting officer issuing a women-owned small business set-aside may award the contract only to a WOSB-certified vendor. If your organization qualifies and you have not certified, you cannot compete — no matter how strong your proposal. The certification is the entry ticket.

Certifications also signal credibility. A faith-based nonprofit with one or more federal certifications is communicating to the marketplace that it has been vetted, verified, and recognized. That carries weight in a system where trust and track record open doors.

Certifications at a Glance

The table below outlines the major certifications relevant to faith-based organizations. Each one is covered in detail in the sections that follow.

Certification	Who Qualifies	Where to Apply
WOSB	Women-owned small businesses and nonprofits led by women	certify.sba.gov
EDWOSB	Women-owned, economically disadvantaged (lower income/assets)	certify.sba.gov
HUBZone	Located in a Historically Underutilized Business Zone	certify.sba.gov
VOSB	Veteran-owned small business (51%+ veteran-owned/controlled)	vetbiz.va.gov
SDVOSB	Service-disabled veteran-owned small business	vetbiz.va.gov
8(a) Program	Socially and economically disadvantaged small businesses	certify.sba.gov

The SBA Equal Treatment Policy for Faith-Based Organizations

One of the most important policy developments for faith-based nonprofits entering the federal marketplace is a principle reinforced across multiple administrations: the federal government cannot discriminate against an organization on the basis of religion when awarding contracts or grants. This means your faith identity — the crosses on the wall, the prayer before staff meetings, the biblical framework underlying your approach to service — does not disqualify you from federal funding.

The Small Business Administration has specifically affirmed that faith-based organizations are eligible to apply for and receive SBA certifications on the same basis as any other nonprofit or small business. There is no faith exemption in the certification system that works against you. The eligibility requirements are the same across the board — size, ownership structure, location, and financial status — and none of them exclude religious identity.

What this means in practice: if your organization meets the numerical and structural criteria for certification, apply. Do not assume the federal government will see your faith identity as a barrier. The law says otherwise, and the policy has been consistently applied in your favor.

WOSB and EDWOSB: Women-Owned Small Business Certifications

The Women-Owned Small Business (WOSB) certification is one of the most widely used set-aside designations in federal contracting. Congress has mandated that five percent of all federal contracting dollars go to women-owned small businesses annually. Agencies work actively to meet that goal, which means contracting officers are looking for WOSB-certified vendors. Being certified puts your organization in a pool that agencies are motivated to use.

To qualify as a WOSB, your organization must meet two conditions. First, it must qualify as a small business under the SBA's size standards for your primary NAICS code. Most faith-based nonprofits will meet this threshold comfortably. Second, the organization must be at least 51 percent owned and controlled by one or more US citizen women. For a faith-based nonprofit, 'control' means the woman or women in leadership have day-to-day management authority and make long-term strategic decisions. If a woman serves as executive director with genuine decision-making power over organizational direction and operations, this requirement is typically met.

The Economically Disadvantaged Women-Owned Small Business certification — EDWOSB — layers an additional financial criterion on top of WOSB. To qualify, the woman's personal net worth must be less than $850,000, her adjusted gross income over the prior three years must average less than $400,000, and her total assets must be below $6.5 million. EDWOSB set-asides are even more targeted than standard WOSB set-asides, meaning the competition pool is smaller. If you qualify for both, you should hold both certifications.

Both certifications are obtained through the SBA's certification portal at certify.sba.gov. The application requires documentation of ownership structure, leadership authority, and financial information. Plan for the process to take several weeks from submission to approval.

Pro Tip

When applying for WOSB certification, documentation of 'control' is often the most scrutinized part of the application. Gather evidence of day-to-day management authority before you begin: board meeting minutes showing the executive director's decision-making role, organizational charts, employment agreements, and any governance documents that confirm leadership structure. Having these ready before you start the application significantly reduces processing time.

HUBZone: Serving Your Community and Earning Recognition for It

The HUBZone program — Historically Underutilized Business Zone — certifies businesses and nonprofits located in areas that the federal government has identified as economically distressed. HUBZone set-asides carry a significant advantage: agencies can restrict competitions to HUBZone-certified entities, and HUBZone firms receive a 10 percent price evaluation preference in unrestricted competitions.

To qualify, your principal office must be located in a designated HUBZone, and at least 35 percent of your employees must reside in a HUBZone. For faith-based nonprofits already serving in low-income urban neighborhoods, rural communities, or post-industrial areas, this certification may be closer within reach than you realize. Many of the zip codes where ministry organizations have deep roots are HUBZone-designated areas.

You can check whether your address falls within a HUBZone by using the SBA's HUBZone map at certify.sba.gov. Enter your office address and the tool will tell you immediately whether you are in a qualifying zone. If you are, this certification should be near the top of your list — it is one of the few that gives you a price advantage in open competitions, not just access to set-asides.

Veteran-Owned Certifications: VOSB and SDVOSB

Two certifications serve veteran-led organizations: the Veteran-Owned Small Business (VOSB) designation and the Service-Disabled Veteran-Owned Small Business (SDVOSB) designation. Both certifications are verified through the SBA's Veteran Small Business Certification program at vetbiz.va.gov, which took over the certification function from the VA in 2023.

To qualify as a VOSB, your organization must be at least 51 percent owned and controlled by one or more veterans. The veteran or veterans must be US citizens and must hold the highest officer position in the organization. Control is defined similarly to the WOSB standard — day-to-day management authority and long-term decision-making power must rest with the qualifying veteran. SDVOSB adds the requirement that the controlling veteran has a service-connected disability rating from the VA or the Department of Defense.

For faith-based organizations in communities near military installations, these certifications carry particular weight. Areas surrounding major installations often have significant veteran density, and a veteran-led faith organization in those communities that holds VOSB or SDVOSB certification is well-positioned to pursue VA contracts, Department of Defense community programs, and agency-specific veteran support initiatives set aside for veteran-owned entities.

Even if the founding leader of your organization is not a veteran, review your leadership team and board. If a veteran holds a qualifying ownership or controlling leadership position, that may be sufficient to establish eligibility depending on organizational structure. The SBA's eligibility guidance at certify.sba.gov provides detailed criteria for nonprofit structures.

The 8(a) Business Development Program

The SBA's 8(a) Business Development Program is a nine-year certification designed for small businesses owned by socially and economically disadvantaged individuals. The program provides participants with set-aside contract opportunities, sole-source contract awards, and mentorship through the SBA. Participants in the 8(a) program have access to contracting opportunities unavailable in the general marketplace.

To qualify, the business must be owned and controlled by an individual or individuals who are both socially disadvantaged — belonging to a group that has faced racial, ethnic, or cultural bias — and economically disadvantaged, with personal net worth below $750,000 and total assets below $6 million. Many founders of faith-based nonprofits serving historically marginalized communities will meet both criteria.

The 8(a) application process is more involved than other certifications and typically takes three to six months from submission to approval. However, the benefits are substantial — 8(a) participants can receive sole-source contract awards up to $4.5 million for goods and services without competing at all, as long as the awarding agency determines the price is fair and reasonable. For a faith-based organization that has developed specialized expertise in a particular service area, this is one of the most powerful doors in the federal system.

Registering Certifications in SAM.gov

Certifications earned through the SBA or VA are typically reflected in your SAM.gov profile automatically once approved, because those systems communicate with each other. However, you should verify this manually. Log in to SAM.gov after receiving your certification approval, navigate to your entity profile, and confirm that the certification appears in your Representations and Certifications section.

If a certification does not appear automatically, you can add it manually during your next SAM.gov update cycle. In the Representations and Certifications section, you will be asked to self-certify whether your organization meets various criteria. Review each question carefully and answer based on your verified certification status. The SBA-managed certifications will populate from the federal database; self-certifications require you to attest to your own eligibility.

Keep your certifications current. Most have annual or biennial renewal requirements. A lapsed certification can disqualify your organization from a set-aside opportunity even if you qualified at the time of award. Build renewal dates into your organizational calendar the same way you track your SAM.gov registration expiration.

Watch Out

Do not self-certify as WOSB, EDWOSB, or SDVOSB in SAM.gov without first going through the formal SBA or VA certification process. While SAM.gov may allow you to check a box, unverified self-certifications can expose your organization to legal liability if challenged by a competitor or an inspector general review. Always get the formal certification first, then update SAM.gov to reflect it.

Real Talk

One certification applied correctly is worth more than five listed carelessly. If you hold a WOSB certification and you are competing in a WOSB set-aside, you are one of a smaller pool of competitors — that is a real advantage. But if you self-certify without verification, or hold a certification you no longer meet the requirements for, you are creating a liability, not an asset. Certify honestly. Renew diligently. Compete confidently.

Closing Action

Review the certifications in this chapter against your organization's leadership structure, location, and financial profile. Identify every certification your organization may qualify for. For each one, write down the application website, the key eligibility requirements to verify, and a target date for completing the application. Then log in to SAM.gov and confirm that your current certification status is accurate. Start with the one you are most likely to qualify for and submit that application first.

You now know how to classify your work with NAICS codes and how to signal your eligibility through certifications. The next step is finding the actual opportunities — the solicitations, grants, and contract vehicles that are waiting to be matched with organizations like yours. Chapter 7 introduces the federal marketplace search tools and shows you how to search with precision.

— End of Chapter 6 —

PART THREE | THE PORTALS

CHAPTER SEVEN

Your Three Essential Portals: SAM.gov, Grants.gov & USASpending.gov

"Where do I even find opportunities that match my mission?"

The federal government doesn't hide its money. Every opportunity — every grant, every contract, every open solicitation — is publicly posted, available to any organization willing to look. The challenge is not access. The challenge is knowing where to look, what to look for, and how to tell the difference between a program that fits your ministry and one that only appears to. Diana spent weeks searching the internet for government grants before someone finally told her there were three specific portals where virtually everything is posted. Three websites. That's it. Nobody had told her.

This chapter introduces all three, walks you through what each one is for, and shows you how to use them together as a system. By the time you finish, you will have bookmarked all three portals, run your first real searches, and identified at least one program that already exists to fund the work you are doing.

The Three Portals at a Glance

Portal	What It Is	Best For	Website
SAM.gov	Federal contracting marketplace — all contract opportunities posted here by law	Finding contracts, set-asides, and Sources Sought notices	sam.gov
Grants.gov	Federal grant and cooperative agreement portal — competitive grants from all agencies	Searching for grant opportunities; submitting applications	grants.gov
USASpending.gov	Federal spending database — shows who has already received funding and for what	Competitive research: identifying target agencies and partners	usaspending.gov

SAM.gov — The Contracting Portal

SAM.gov is the System for Award Management, the single mandatory posting location for all federal contract opportunities.

Federal law requires agencies to post solicitations on SAM.gov, which means if you are looking for federal contracts, this is your starting point — not a search engine, not a third-party site, not a newsletter. SAM.gov.

To search for contract opportunities, go to sam.gov and select Contract Opportunities from the navigation. From there, you can search by keyword, NAICS code, agency, location, or set-aside type. Start with a keyword search using language that describes your programs — 'youth services,' 'housing navigation,' 'workforce development,' 'substance abuse treatment,' 'emergency food.' Review the results and notice which agencies are issuing solicitations in those areas. Those agencies should go on your target list.

The set-aside filter is one of the most valuable tools available to a certified organization. If you hold a WOSB, HUBZone, SDVOSB, or small business certification, you can filter for set-aside opportunities reserved for organizations with your designation. This significantly narrows the pool of competitors and surfaces contracts that only organizations with your status can win.

Pay close attention to the notice type. SAM.gov posts several kinds of notices, and they are not all the same. A Presolicitation notice announces that a solicitation is coming — it's your early warning to start preparing. A Sources Sought notice is market research: the agency is asking who's out there before they write the contract. Responding to Sources Sought puts your name in front of the contracting officer before anyone has competed for anything — that is, relationship-building, not competition. A Combined Synopsis/Solicitation is the actual contract opportunity, fully posted and open for proposals. An Award Notice tells you who won a contract that has already been awarded — useful for competitive research but not actionable on its own.

Create a free account on SAM.gov and save your searches. The system will email you notifications when new opportunities match your criteria. This turns the portal from a tool you visit into a system that works for you.

Grants.gov — The Grants Portal

Grants.gov is the federal government's centralized portal for competitive grants and most cooperative agreements. Every federal agency is required to post competitive grant opportunities here, making it a single search point for grant funding across the entire federal government — HUD, HHS, DOL, FEMA, USDA, DOJ, and dozens more.

Search on Grants.gov by keyword, agency, Assistance Listing Number (formerly called the CFDA number), or eligibility type. The eligibility filter is particularly important for faith-based organizations: select 'Nonprofits having a 501(c)(3) status with the IRS, other than institutions of higher education' and 'Faith-Based and Community Organizations' to narrow results to opportunities your organization qualifies for. Using both filters together removes the noise and surfaces only what applies to you.

Set up email alerts on Grants.gov. Enter your keywords and saved search criteria, and the system will notify you when new opportunities are posted that match your profile. Grant deadlines are firm — there are no extensions and no late submissions. Staying current through alerts is not optional; it is the difference between being aware of an opportunity and missing it entirely.

Note that submitting applications through Grants.gov requires a separate Grants.gov registration, distinct from your SAM.gov registration. You will need a Grants.gov organizational account linked to your UEI number before you can submit. Set this up now, before you need it. Registrations can take time to process, and attempting to register the week before a deadline is a common and costly mistake.

USASpending.gov — Your Competitive Intelligence Tool

USASpending.gov is not an application portal. It is a transparency database that shows every dollar the federal government has awarded — to whom, from which agency, under which program, and for what purpose. It is the most underutilized research tool in the federal marketplace and is completely free.

Here is how to use it strategically. Search for nonprofit organizations in your city, county, or state that are doing work similar to yours. Look at their award records: Which agencies funded them? Under which programs? Using which NAICS codes? What was the award amount, and over what period of time? This tells you — with real data — which federal agencies are already investing in your mission area and in your geographic region. Those agencies are your primary targets.

USASpending.gov also surfaces potential teaming partners. If a larger organization in your area is already receiving federal funding in your space, they may be looking for community-based subcontractors with local relationships and specialized expertise. That is often how faith-based organizations enter the federal marketplace for the first time — not as prime contractors winning their own awards, but as subcontractors supporting a prime that is already funded. USASpending.gov shows you who those primes are.

Spend fifteen minutes on USASpending.gov before every application you submit. Search for recent awards in your program area. Review what was funded and how it was described. This is competitive intelligence — use it.

Federal Programs Already Designed for Faith-Based Organizations

Beyond the general search tools, there are specific federal programs with a long track record of partnering with faith-based and community organizations. These programs are worth knowing by name because they represent funding that has been channeled through faith-based partners for years and remains available. The table below covers the most significant ones across HUD, HHS, DOL, and FEMA.

Agency	Program	Best Fit For
HUD	**Continuum of Care (CoC)**	Homelessness prevention and housing: nonprofits as primary partners
HUD	**HOME Investment Partnerships**	Affordable housing construction and rehab; nonprofit set-asides
HUD	**Community Development Block Grant (CDBG)**	Community development: contact your local government to participate
HUD	**Self-Help Homeownership (SHOP)**	Sweat equity homeownership programs for low-income families
HUD	**HOPWA**	Housing for persons with HIV/AIDS; nonprofit partnerships
HUD	**Resident Opportunities & Self-Sufficiency (ROSS)**	Community empowerment and resident self-sufficiency programs

Agency	Program	Best Fit For
HUD	**Section 811**	Housing for persons with disabilities; nonprofit developers
HUD	**Emergency Housing Vouchers (EHV)**	Domestic violence survivors, trafficking victims, and those experiencing homelessness
HUD	**Youth Homelessness Demonstration Program (YHDP)**	Community coalitions addressing youth homelessness
HUD	**Emergency Solutions Grants (ESG)**	Street outreach, emergency shelter, rapid rehousing
HUD	**HUD-VASH**	Housing for homeless veterans; faith-based organizations serve as community partners
HHS	**TIEH**	Mental health and substance use treatment for people experiencing homelessness
DOL	**HVRP (~$65.5M/year)**	Veteran employment reintegration: approximately 160 grants awarded annually
FEMA	**Emergency Food and Shelter**	Hunger and homelessness supplemental funding through local boards

Using All Three Portals as a System

The three portals are most powerful when you use them together rather than independently. Here is the workflow that turns three separate tools into a coordinated research and pursuit system.

Start with USASpending.gov. Before you search for new opportunities, spend fifteen minutes researching who is already funded in your mission area and region. Identify two or three agencies that have recently awarded grants or contracts for work similar to yours. Write those agencies down — they are your targets.

Then move to SAM.gov. Search for contract opportunities from your target agencies using your primary NAICS code and mission-related keywords. Apply the set-aside filter if you hold a relevant certification. Save the search and set up email alerts. Look specifically for Sources Sought notices from your target agencies — responding to Sources Sought is one of the fastest ways to get your organization's name in front of a contracting officer before a competition opens.

Then move to Grants.gov. Search for grant opportunities from your target agencies using the same keywords. Filter by eligibility to narrow results to what you actually qualify for. Save the search and set up email alerts. Note deadlines immediately and add them to your calendar, with a preparation timeline that works backward from the due date.

Return to all three portals weekly. The federal marketplace moves constantly — new opportunities post, deadlines pass, agencies shift priorities. Organizations that check in regularly are the ones that catch opportunities early enough to prepare competitive applications. Those who only search when they need funding usually arrive too late.

Pro Tip

On USASpending.gov, search for award recipients in your city or county doing work similar to yours. Look at what they're doing and which agencies are funding them. This fifteen-minute research session will tell you more about your local federal funding landscape than hours of general browsing — and it will show you which agencies are already investing in your community.

Watch Out

Faith-based organizations near military installations should search specifically for HUD-VASH and DOL HVRP opportunities on both SAM.gov and Grants.gov. These programs are among the most heavily funded in communities with significant veteran populations, and federal agencies actively seek community-based faith partners in those areas. If your ministry serves veterans or their families, these programs belong at the top of your search list.

Real Talk

You do not need a grant writer to search these portals. You need fifteen minutes and an internet connection. Start there. The opportunities that match your mission are already posted — they are waiting for you to find them. Search first. Then we talk about how to respond.

Closing Action

Bookmark all three portals today: sam.gov, grants.gov, and usaspending.gov. Run one search in each portal using your primary NAICS code or a keyword that describes your ministry's core service. On USASpending.gov, find one organization in your area that is already receiving federal funding for work similar to yours and note which agency funded them. Write down the name of at least one program or opportunity relevant to your ministry, the agency behind it, and its program number or Assistance Listing Number.

You know where the portals are, and you have run your first searches. Now it's time to become a skilled searcher — because how you search determines what you find. Chapter 8 moves you from browsing to pursuing, with targeted search strategies that surface the right opportunities for your specific ministry rather than a flood of results that don't fit.

— End of Chapter 7 —

PART THREE | THE PORTALS

CHAPTER EIGHT

Searching for Opportunities That Match Your Mission

"How do I find the RIGHT opportunities for my specific ministry?"

There are thousands of federal opportunities posted every week. You cannot read them all — and you shouldn't try. What you need is a search system that filters the noise, surfaces the signal, and delivers relevant opportunities to your inbox before the deadline passes. The portals are open. The opportunities are there. This chapter is about learning to search with precision so that you stop finding everything and start finding what's actually yours.

Building Your Keyword Library

Every search starts with a word. The words you choose determine what comes back — and what doesn't. The most common mistake faith-based organizations make when searching federal portals is to use the language they use internally for their own work, rather than the language a contracting officer or program officer uses externally.

Think like the person on the other side of the desk. A contracting officer issuing a solicitation for youth mentoring services is not writing the words 'saving the next generation' in the contract description. They are writing 'out-of-school time services,' 'youth development,' 'positive youth outcomes,' or 'at-risk youth intervention.' Those are the words you need to search. The mission is the same. The language is different.

Start by listing every word or phrase that describes what your organization does, who you serve, and the outcomes you produce. Write them all down — this is your keyword library, and it is the foundation of your entire search strategy. Then translate each internal phrase into outcome-focused, service-delivery language that appears in federal solicitations. The two columns below show that translation in practice.

How Your Ministry Describes It	How to Search the Federal Portals
Feeding the hungry	Food security services, nutritional assistance, emergency food distribution
Youth ministry / after-school	Out-of-school time, youth development, at-risk youth, academic support
Helping the homeless	Homelessness prevention, rapid rehousing, street outreach, shelter services
Counseling ministry	Behavioral health, community counseling, mental health services
Helping ex-offenders	Reentry services, justice-involved individuals, workforce reintegration

How Your Ministry Describes It	How to Search the Federal Portals
Veterans' ministry	Veteran reintegration, veteran support services, wraparound case management
Housing assistance	Housing stability, housing navigation, affordable housing, transitional housing
Drug and alcohol recovery	Substance use disorder treatment, recovery support services, MOUD

Test each keyword in both SAM.gov and Grants.gov. The same mission area may use slightly different language across the two portals — contract solicitations tend toward service-delivery terminology, while grant opportunities sometimes use program or policy language. Build a library of ten to fifteen terms and use them in combination to cast a wide but targeted net.

Step-by-Step

Build your keyword library right now: Open a notes document and list every word or phrase that describes (1) what your organization does, (2) who you serve, and (3) the outcomes you deliver. Then translate each item into federal search language using the table above as a guide. That list is your search engine. Use it every time you open SAM.gov or Grants.gov.

Assistance Listing Numbers — The Grant-Seeker's Shortcut

Every federal assistance program — every grant program funded by a federal agency — is assigned a unique Assistance Listing Number, also known as an ALN. You may still see these referred to as CFDA numbers, which stand for Catalog of Federal Domestic Assistance. The naming has changed; the function has not. The ALN is a five-digit number (formatted as XX.XXX) that identifies a specific federal grant program across all agencies and across all years.

Once you find a grant program that matches your mission, write down its ALN immediately. That number is your direct line back to that program in every future funding cycle. Rather than searching by keyword and filtering through hundreds of results, you can search Grants.gov or the SAM Assistance Listings database by ALN and go directly to every opportunity under that specific program — past, current, and upcoming.

A few ALNs worth knowing for faith-based organizations serving vulnerable populations: the HUD Continuum of Care program is listed under ALN 14.267. HUD's Emergency Solutions Grants program is 14.231. HHS's Transitional Living Program for Homeless Youth is 93.550. The DOL Homeless Veterans Reintegration Program is 17.805. Bookmark these. Add them to your keyword library. The next time any of these programs posts a new funding cycle, you will find it in seconds rather than minutes.

Set-Aside Filters — Finding What's Already Reserved for You

A set-aside opportunity is one where the competition has already been narrowed by design. Federal agencies are required to set aside a portion of their contracting dollars for specific categories of vendors — small businesses, women-owned small businesses, HUBZone-certified entities, service-disabled veteran-owned businesses. When you filter for set-asides, you are not reducing the universe of available opportunities. You are finding the ones where the field is already restricted to organizations like yours.

On SAM.gov, use the Set-Aside Type filter in the Contract Opportunities search. You can filter for Small Business, WOSB, EDWOSB, HUBZone, SDVOSB, and 8(a) set-asides individually or in combination. Run this filter every time you search. A set-aside solicitation with five eligible organizations responding is a fundamentally different competitive environment than an unrestricted solicitation with five hundred.

On Grants.gov, the equivalent filter is the Eligibility field. Select 'Nonprofits having a 501(c)(3) status with the IRS, other than institutions of higher education' as your baseline. Add 'Faith-Based and Community Organizations' as a second filter. These two eligibility categories together surface the grant opportunities that your organization qualifies for and that are actively designed to include partners like you.

Saved Searches and Email Alerts

Searching the portals once is research. Setting up saved searches is building a system. The difference is that a system works for you whether you remember to check or not.

On SAM.gov, run your search with your preferred keyword and filter combinations, then save it using the Save Search option at the top of the results page. Give it a clear name — 'Youth Services WOSB Set-Aside' or 'Housing Navigation HHS' — so you can identify it at a glance. Then set the notification frequency to daily or weekly. SAM.gov will email you whenever a new opportunity matches your saved search criteria.

On Grants.gov, create a saved search from the Advanced Search page. Enter your keywords, select your eligibility filters, and choose your preferred notification settings. Grants.gov will email you when new funding opportunities matching your search are posted. Given that grant application deadlines are often 30 to 60 days after posting — and preparation for a competitive grant application can easily take 2 to 3 weeks — early notification is not a convenience. It is a competitive advantage.

Create a dedicated email folder for federal opportunity alerts. When notifications arrive, review them the same day and flag anything worth evaluating further. Make it a standing weekly practice — Monday morning, 15 minutes — to review your alerts and update your opportunity calendar. Organizations that build this habit consistently find opportunities. Those who only search when they need funding usually find out about the right opportunities too late to respond.

How to Evaluate an Opportunity Before Investing Time

Not every opportunity that matches your keywords is an opportunity worth pursuing. Federal applications take time — sometimes significant time — and chasing the wrong opportunities is one of the fastest ways to burn out a team and lose momentum. Before you commit to pursuing anything, run it through a quick five-question evaluation.

Evaluation Question	Yes → Keep Going	No → Move On
Do we actually do this work?	Add to your opportunity calendar	This is not your opportunity

Evaluation Question	Yes → Keep Going	No → Move On
Are we eligible to apply?	Confirm certification/status match	Don't waste time on a disqualifier
Can we meet the deadline?	Start your preparation timeline	A rushed application rarely wins
Do we have the capacity to deliver?	Assess honestly — overcommitting costs more than passing	A contract you can't perform harms your record
Is the award size worth the effort?	Calculate your cost to apply vs. the award value	Some opportunities cost more to pursue than they pay

If any answer is no, move on — and move on without guilt. Not every opportunity is your opportunity, and knowing the difference is a skill, not a failure. Your time and your team's energy are finite. Investing them in the right opportunities is strategic. Chasing every opportunity that sounds adjacent to your mission is exhausting and rarely productive.

Building Your Opportunity Calendar

Every opportunity you decide to pursue should go on a calendar — not just as a deadline, but as a project with a timeline working backward from that deadline. A federal grant with a sixty-day application window does not give you sixty days to write a proposal. It gives you roughly 45 days, once you account for the time needed to gather attachments, obtain organizational sign-offs, register on the submission portal, and review the final package before submitting.

For each opportunity on your calendar, track the opportunity name, the issuing agency, the deadline, the estimated award amount, the NAICS code or ALN, and your next action step. Review the calendar every Monday when you check your portal alerts. What needs attention this week? What deadline is 30 days out and hasn't been started yet? What have you already submitted and are waiting to hear about?

Many federal grant programs run on annual cycles — the same program posts new funding at roughly the same time each year. Once you have applied to a program once, you know its cycle. Plan for it. Begin your preparation before the solicitation even posts, based on last year's requirements. Organizations that approach the federal marketplace as a pipeline rather than a series of one-time applications are the ones that build sustainable, recurring funding relationships with federal agencies.

Pro Tip

When you find a grant program whose cycle you want to track, look up last year's solicitation on Grants.gov and note when it posted. Set a calendar reminder two months before that same date next year. You will have your keyword library, your capability statement, and your eligibility documentation ready before most organizations know the solicitation has opened.

Real Talk

A common temptation is to pursue every opportunity that mentions your population — homeless, veterans, youth, and food-insecure. Resist it. Submitting three strong, targeted, well-prepared applications is more likely to result in awards than submitting ten rushed ones. Build a short list. Prepare well. Submit with confidence.

Closing Action

Set up at least two saved searches today — one on SAM.gov and one on Grants.gov. Use your primary NAICS code and two keywords from your ministry's core service area. Confirm that email notifications are turned on for both. Then open a spreadsheet or notes document and create your opportunity calendar with these columns: Opportunity Name, Agency, Deadline, Award Amount, ALN or NAICS, Next Action. Check your alerts next Monday and add anything relevant.

Your search system is built. Opportunities are coming to you. When a Sources Sought notice lands in your inbox — or when you decide to reach out to an agency proactively — you will need a document that introduces your organization with precision and makes a contracting officer remember you. That document is your capability statement. Chapter 9 builds it from scratch.

— End of Chapter 8 —

PART THREE | THE PORTALS

CHAPTER NINE

Writing Your Capability Statement as a Faith-Based Organization

"What is a capability statement and how do I write one?"

A capability statement is your federal one-pager — one page that tells a contracting officer everything they need to know about your organization in the time it takes to drink a cup of coffee. It is not a brochure. It is not a grant proposal. It is not your annual report, your newsletter, or your church bulletin. It is a precision document that answers three questions as efficiently as possible: What do you do? Can you prove it? How do I reach you?

Diana had been doing extraordinary work for over twenty years — feeding families, sheltering women, training young people for jobs. She had outcomes, partnerships, and a story worth telling. What she didn't have was a document that translated all of that into the language a contracting officer would recognize, trust, and file for later. This chapter helps you write that document. By the time you finish, you will have a draft you can actually use.

What a Capability Statement Is and When You Use It

A capability statement is a one-page marketing document that introduces your organization to federal contracting officers, grant program managers, and prime contractors. It is the federal marketplace equivalent of a business card — except it contains everything a decision-maker needs to evaluate whether your organization is worth a conversation.

You use it in four specific situations. First, when responding to a Sources Sought notice, agencies often request capability statements as part of their market research before writing a solicitation. Submitting a strong one puts your name on the contracting officer's radar before any competition opens. Second, industry days and matchmaking events are sessions where agencies introduce upcoming contract opportunities and meet potential vendors. You should never attend one without a capability statement in hand. Third, when reaching out to prime contractors, large organizations with federal contracts are often looking for qualified subcontractors in specific geographic areas or service categories. Your capability statement is your introduction. Fourth, when submitting an unsolicited introduction to an agency you want to target, not every federal relationship starts with a formal solicitation. Some start with a well-timed, well-crafted one-pager.

Update your capability statement at least once a year and whenever you add a new program area, a new certification, or a significant past performance example. A document with outdated program descriptions or missing certifications sends the wrong signal to an audience that values accuracy.

The Six Elements of Every Capability Statement

Every effective capability statement contains six elements. None of them is optional. Together, they give a contracting officer or prime contractor everything they need to assess your organization quickly and fit you for the right opportunity.

#	Element	What to Include
1	**Core Competencies**	Your top 3–5 service areas in concise bullet points. These should use federal service language, not ministry language. Lead with what you deliver, not what you believe.
2	**Past Performance**	3–5 examples of work you have delivered, written with specifics: who you served, how many, what outcomes, over what period, and with what partners or funders.
3	**Differentiators**	What makes your organization uniquely qualified. This is where your faith identity, community relationships, certifications, geographic reach, and specialized expertise belong.
4	**Company Data**	UEI number, CAGE code, primary and secondary NAICS codes, active certifications, entity type (nonprofit, faith-based organization), and year established.
5	**Contact Information**	Name, title, phone number, email address, and website of the person who handles federal inquiries. Make it easy to reach the right person immediately.
6	**Branding**	Your organization's logo, name, and brand colors. The capability statement should look like it came from your organization — professional, consistent, and recognizable.

Adapting the Format for Faith-Based Organizations

Faith-based organizations often approach the capability statement with one of two mistakes. The first is writing it as a ministry document — full of mission language, scripture references, and testimonials that speak to donors but mean nothing to a contracting officer. The second is scrubbing every trace of faith identity out of the document in an attempt to look 'more like a regular business' — and losing the strongest differentiators in the process.

The right approach is both simpler and more strategic. Keep your faith identity in the Differentiators section, where it belongs. Community trust built over decades, volunteer networks that extend your reach without adding to your overhead, decades of relationship-based service in neighborhoods that federal agencies have difficulty penetrating on their own — these are genuine competitive advantages. Name them plainly. 'Faith-based organization with 22 years of embedded community relationships in [City/County]' tells a contracting officer something real and useful.

At the same time, keep religious language out of your Core Competencies and Past Performance sections. Those sections are read by people who are evaluating your service delivery capability, not your theology. Write them in outcome-focused, service-delivery language. The programs you run may be motivated by faith. The results they produce — the meals served, the families housed, the veterans employed — are measurable and should be described that way.

Your faith identity is an asset in this marketplace. Use it where it strengthens your case, and step out of the way where it doesn't add value to the evaluator's decision.

Translating Ministry Work into Contracting Language

The single most important writing skill for a capability statement is translation — taking the language your community uses to describe your work and converting it into the language a contracting officer uses to search for vendors. The work itself does not change. The description does.

Ministry Description	Capability Statement Language
Feeding the hungry	Food security and nutritional support services for low-income households
Youth ministry / after-school program	Out-of-school time youth development and academic support services
Helping the homeless	Homelessness prevention, rapid rehousing, and emergency shelter services
Counseling ministry	Behavioral health and community counseling services
Helping ex-offenders get back on their feet	Reentry support services and workforce reintegration for justice-involved individuals
Veterans ministry	Veteran reintegration support and wraparound case management services
Housing assistance	Housing stability navigation and emergency housing referral services
Drug and alcohol recovery support	Substance use disorder recovery support and community-based treatment navigation

Use this translation discipline throughout your capability statement — in your core competencies, past performance descriptions, and differentiators. You are not changing what you do. You are making sure that the person reading your document can immediately connect your work to the solicitations and programs they manage.

> **Example**
>
> Past Performance entry for a faith-based food ministry: "New Vision Community Ministries provided weekly food security services to 1,200+ food-insecure residents over three years in partnership with the County Department of Social Services. Distributed more than 150,000 meals with a 98% client satisfaction rate. Program operated at zero administrative cost to the county through volunteer coordination infrastructure."

Common Mistakes to Avoid

The capability statement is a short document, but it is easy to get wrong. These are the mistakes that most commonly undermine an otherwise strong organization's first impression in the federal marketplace.

Making it longer than one page is the most common error. The format exists for a reason — a contracting officer at an industry day may receive fifty capability statements in a single morning. If yours runs to two pages, it signals that you don't understand the marketplace. One page. That is the standard.

Using ministry or church language without translation is a close second. Words like 'blessed,' 'anointed,' 'called,' 'ministry,' and 'congregation' may resonate deeply in your community, but they do not translate into the evaluative language of a federal procurement.

Save those words for your donor communications. Your capability statement needs to speak the contracting officer's language.

Leaving out your UEI number and CAGE code is a practical error that creates friction. These identifiers are what connect your capability statement to your SAM.gov record. A contracting officer who wants to follow up on your organization will search by UEI. If it's not on the document, they have an extra step — and that extra step is often the one that doesn't happen.

Using outdated past performance examples weakens your credibility. Federal agencies look for evidence of recent, relevant delivery. Keep your examples within the last three to five years whenever possible, and update the document whenever you complete a significant program or add a new funding relationship.

Finally, omitting your certifications is one of the most expensive omissions you can make. Your certifications are competitive differentiators. A contracting officer reviewing your capability statement for a set-aside opportunity needs to see at a glance that you hold the relevant certification. List your active certifications in the Company Data section, and consider renaming them in your Differentiators. They are not fine print — they are a headline.

Pro Tip

See Appendix C for a ready-to-use Capability Statement Template sized and formatted for faith-based organizations. Fill in your organization's information across all six elements, and you will have a document ready to submit, share, or hand out at your next industry day or agency meeting.

Closing Action
Draft your capability statement using the Appendix C template. Work through all six elements: core competencies, past performance, differentiators, company data, contact information, and branding. When you have a complete draft, ask someone outside your organization to read it and summarize what your organization does in one sentence. If their summary is accurate, your capability statement is doing its job. If it isn't, revise the core competencies until it is.

Your capability statement is ready. Your search alerts are running. Now comes the moment Diana has been building toward — a Sources Sought notice just landed in her inbox. She knows what it is. She knows why it matters. Chapter 10 shows her exactly what to do next, step by step, from the moment she opens the notice to the moment she submits her response.

— End of Chapter 9 —

PART THREE | THE PORTALS

CHAPTER TEN

Responding to Sources Sought Notices and RFPs

"Someone sent me a Sources Sought — what do I do?"

You found it. A Sources Sought notice posted on SAM.gov from an agency that funds exactly the kind of work you do—the NAICS code matches. The population matches. The geographic area matches. Your heart is racing. And you have absolutely no idea what to do next.

Here is the first thing to know: a Sources Sought is not a contract. It is not a solicitation. It is not a competition. It is an invitation. The agency is asking a question — 'who's out there?' — before they write the actual contract. Responding costs you nothing but time. It obligates you to nothing. And it gets your organization's name in front of the contracting officer before anyone else has started preparing a bid. This chapter shows you exactly how to respond — and how to do it in a way that makes the agency want to see more of you.

What a Sources Sought Is — and What It Isn't

A Sources Sought notice is market research. Federal agencies are required to understand the vendor landscape before issuing a solicitation. Specifically, they need to know whether there are enough qualified small businesses or certified vendors in a given area to justify a set-aside. A Sources Sought is how they find out.

It is not a contract offer. Submitting a response does not put you under any legal obligation, does not guarantee you will receive a future solicitation, and does not mean you have won anything. What it means is that the contracting officer now knows your organization exists, what you do, and has your contact information on file when the solicitation is written.

Failing to respond to a relevant Sources Sought is one of the most common and most costly passive mistakes in the federal marketplace. If the agency issues a Sources Sought for youth development services in your county and your organization does not respond, the contracting officer has no evidence that you exist. They may determine that there are not enough certified nonprofits in the area to justify a set-aside and write a full and open competition that gives you no advantage. Your response to a Sources Sought is not just a reply to a notice. It is evidence that shapes the wording of the solicitation.

Watch Out

Sources Sought windows are short — typically seven to fourteen days after posting. If you have saved searches and email alerts set up on SAM.gov, you will catch these notices in time to respond. If you are only checking the portal occasionally, you will miss them. This is one of the strongest arguments for building the weekly review habit covered in Chapter 8.

Why Your Response Matters Even When Nothing Happens Immediately

The federal marketplace runs on relationships built incrementally over time. Most organizations that win federal contracts do not win them on their first response to a Sources Sought notice. They win them the third or fourth time — after the contracting officer has seen their name consistently, after a program manager has read their capability statement twice, after they responded thoughtfully to a notice that ultimately went nowhere.

Every Sources Sought response you submit is a touchpoint. It puts your name in the contracting officer's awareness. It demonstrates that your organization is engaged, monitoring the marketplace, and ready to respond when called. Agencies notice this. When the actual solicitation posts and the contracting officer is evaluating proposals, the name they recognize from a previous Sources Sought response starts with a layer of familiarity that a completely unknown organization does not have.

Additionally, your certifications are particularly important at the Sources Sought stage. When agencies receive responses, they assess whether there are enough WOSB-certified vendors, HUBZone organizations, and small businesses to support a set-aside. Your response — with your certifications clearly stated — is a direct input into that decision. If you hold a WOSB certification and the agency receives three WOSB responses, including yours, they now have evidence to justify a WOSB set-aside that benefits you. If you don't respond, that evidence doesn't exist.

How to Read a Sources Sought Notice

Before you write a single word of your response, read the entire Sources Sought notice carefully. Most notices are one to three pages. Every sentence in them is intentional. Here is what to look for.

Identify the agency and the program. Who is issuing this notice, and what program are they planning to fund? Understanding the agency's mission and the specific program context tells you how to frame your response — what to emphasize, which past performance examples are most relevant, and what language to use.

Find the NAICS code. Confirm it matches one of your registered codes in SAM.gov. If it doesn't, you may still be able to respond, but note the discrepancy — and use this as a reminder to update your NAICS codes if they describe work you actually do.

Read the specific questions. Most Sources Sought notices ask between two and five specific questions. These questions are the heart of the notice, and answering every single one of them — in the order they are asked — is the most important thing you will do in your response. Common questions include: Does your organization provide this type of service? What is your organization's size and certification status? Do you have relevant past performance? What is your geographic reach or service area? The questions tell you exactly what the agency is trying to learn. Answer them directly.

Note the deadline and the point of contact. The deadline is firm — there are no extensions on Sources Sought responses. The point of contact is the contracting officer or specialist managing this notice. This is the person you are writing to. Keep their role in mind as you draft your response.

The Anatomy of a Strong Sources Sought Response

A Sources Sought response does not need to be long. It needs to be clear, complete, and professional. The structure below covers every element a strong response should contain.

Section	What to Write
Header	Organization name, UEI number, CAGE code, primary NAICS code, active certifications (WOSB, HUBZone, SDVOSB, etc.), and point-of-contact name and email.
Introduction	One paragraph: who you are, what you do, where you operate, and why this specific opportunity is relevant to your organization's mission and experience.
Response to Agency Questions	Answer each question from the notice directly and in the order asked. Do not combine answers or reorder questions. Agencies check for responsiveness to every item.
Past Performance	Two to three relevant examples. For each: program name, funding source or partner agency, scope of work, population served, and measurable outcome.
Closing Statement	Express your organization's interest in the anticipated solicitation. Request to be notified when it is posted. Include full contact information for follow-up.

Section	What to Write
Attachment	Your capability statement. Always attach it. This is your organization's full introduction and gives the contracting officer a complete picture beyond what the response covers.

A Response Framework for Faith-Based Organizations

The framework below provides a starting structure you can adapt to any Sources Sought notice. Replace the bracketed fields with your organization's specific information and the agency's specific questions.

Sources Sought Response Framework

ORGANIZATION INFORMATION

Organization Name: [Legal name as registered in SAM.gov]
UEI: [Your UEI number] | CAGE Code: [Your CAGE code]
Primary NAICS: [Your primary NAICS code]
Certifications: [List all active certifications — WOSB, HUBZone, SDVOSB, 8(a), etc.]

INTRODUCTION

[Organization Name] is a [entity type — nonprofit, faith-based organization, etc.] with [X years] of experience providing [core service area] to [target population] in [geographic area]. We are [list certifications] and are actively registered in SAM.gov under UEI [number]. We respectfully submit this response to the Sources Sought notice referenced above.

RESPONSE TO AGENCY QUESTIONS

Question 1: [Copy the agency's exact question here] Response: [Your direct, specific answer]

Question 2: [Copy the agency's exact question here] Response: [Your direct, specific answer]

PAST PERFORMANCE

Example 1: [Program name] — [Funding source or partner agency]. [Scope of work and population served.] [Measurable outcome — number served, timeframe, results.]

Example 2: [Program name] — [Funding source or partner agency]. [Scope of work and population served.] [Measurable outcome.]

CLOSING

[Organization Name] is highly interested in the anticipated solicitation resulting from this Sources Sought. We respectfully request notification when the solicitation is posted. Please find our capability statement attached. For questions, please contact [Name], [Title], at [Phone] or [Email].

RFPs — The Next Level

A Request for Proposal — RFP — is the formal solicitation that typically follows a Sources Sought and a period of market research. Where a Sources Sought asks who can do this work, an RFP asks you to prove that your organization specifically can do it, better than anyone else competing for the same contract. RFPs are longer and more structured, requiring a full written proposal that addresses a detailed set of evaluation criteria.

A full guide to RFP writing is beyond the scope of this book — it is a discipline unto itself that warrants dedicated study and preparation. What you need to know right now is that your Sources Sought responses and your capability statement are the foundation of every proposal you will ever write. The past performance examples you document today, the service descriptions you refine for your capability statement, the relationships you build by responding consistently to Sources Sought notices — all of it feeds directly into your proposal writing capacity when you are ready to compete for full contracts.

In the meantime, if an RFP lands in your inbox before you feel ready, you have options. The APEX Accelerator program — formerly known as the Procurement Technical Assistance Center network — provides free proposal writing assistance to small businesses and nonprofits across the country. Every state has at least one APEX Accelerator location. Contact your local center before you attempt to write your first RFP on your own. The support is free, the guidance is specific, and the difference between a first proposal written alone and one written with professional assistance is often the difference between winning and not placing.

Pro Tip

After you submit a Sources Sought response, follow up. Wait until the response deadline has passed — typically a week to ten days after you submit — then send a brief, professional email to the contracting officer's point of contact. Introduce yourself by name, reference the Sources Sought notice number, confirm your submission, and express your continued interest. One professional follow-up email keeps your name current and demonstrates the kind of proactive engagement that contracting officers remember.

Real Talk

Your first Sources Sought response will not be perfect. That is fine. The agency is not grading it — they are noting that you exist, that you are paying attention, and that you are engaged with the marketplace. A clear, professional response that answers every question is all you need. The goal is not perfection. The goal is presence. Send it.

Closing Action

Go to SAM.gov and find one active Sources Sought notice that is relevant to your ministry's primary service area. Read the entire notice. Draft a response using the framework in this chapter — complete every section, attach your capability statement, and submit before the deadline. Write down the agency name, the contracting officer's contact information, the notice number, and the date you submitted. That record is the beginning of your federal relationship log.

You have done the work. You are registered, certified, searching, and responding. The foundation is built. The final section of this book is about what happens after you win — how to stay compliant, build lasting agency relationships, and turn a single award into a sustainable pipeline that funds your ministry's mission for years to come.

— End of Chapter 10 —

PART FOUR | THE PIPELINE

CHAPTER ELEVEN

Compliance, Reporting, and Staying in Good Standing

"What happens after I win something?"

A federal award marks your entry into the work, not your completion of it. The award letter arrives, the excitement is real, and then — almost immediately — the obligations begin. Reporting deadlines. Financial documentation. Annual renewals. Performance standards. None of this is impossible to manage. But none of it can be ignored, and none of it forgives the excuse of not knowing.

The faith-based organizations that build lasting relationships with federal funders are not necessarily the ones with the most sophisticated programs. They are the ones who deliver on their promises, document what they did, report on time, and show up ready to do it again. This chapter tells you exactly what to expect after an award, so you are prepared before it matters — not scrambling after it does.

Post-Award Requirements — What You Agreed To

When you accept a federal award, you are entering into a legal agreement. The Statement of Work — sometimes called the

Performance Work Statement or the Scope of Work — defines what you are being funded to do, how you will do it, what outcomes you are expected to achieve, and over what time period. Read every page of this document before signing. Do not skim it. The requirements that seem minor in the award package are the ones that become compliance issues six months later.

Performance reporting is a standard requirement on virtually every federal award. Most contracts and grants require quarterly or semi-annual progress reports submitted to your contracting officer or grants officer. These reports document what you have done, how many people you have served, what outcomes you have achieved, and whether you are on track against the milestones in your Statement of Work. Late reports — or missing reports — are a compliance violation that can affect your ability to receive future funding.

Financial reporting runs parallel to performance reporting. You will be required to document every dollar of federal funds spent — what it was spent on, when, and how it connects to the approved budget in your award. Some awards require monthly financial reports; others require quarterly or final reports at close-out. Your grants officer will tell you the frequency. Your job is to maintain records clean enough to produce those reports without scrambling.

If your award involves subcontractors — organizations you are funding to help you deliver the work — you may have additional sub-award reporting obligations. The Federal Funding Accountability and Transparency Act requires prime award recipients to report sub-awards above certain dollar thresholds through SAM.gov. Know your sub-award reporting obligations before you execute any subcontracts.

Annual SAM.gov Renewal — The Non-Negotiable

Your SAM.gov registration expires every twelve months from the date it was last renewed. This is the single most preventable compliance failure in the federal marketplace — and it happens to experienced organizations, not just newcomers. A lapsed SAM.gov registration means you cannot receive payment on any active federal award. It means you cannot be awarded new contracts or grants. It means you are effectively invisible in the federal system until you renew.

Set a calendar reminder sixty days before your SAM.gov expiration date. That gives you time to log in, verify that your information is current, make any necessary updates, and submit your renewal before the expiration creates a problem. The renewal process is the same as the original registration — log into SAM.gov with your Login.gov credentials, navigate to your entity record, review and confirm your information, and resubmit. Processing typically takes seven to ten business days.

Do not wait until the week before your expiration date. Do not assume it will auto-renew. It does not. The renewal is a manual process that requires your active attention, and the ten business days of processing time mean you need to initiate it well before the deadline to avoid a lapse. Treat your SAM.gov renewal date with the same seriousness as a grant deadline — because in terms of your federal standing, it carries equal weight.

Financial Tracking Basics for Nonprofits with Federal Awards

Federal funds must be tracked separately from your organization's other revenue. This is not a suggestion — it is a requirement under federal cost principles, and commingling federal funds with general operating funds is a compliance violation that can result in repayment demands, loss of future funding, and in serious cases, legal liability. Before your first federal dollar arrives, establish a dedicated account or cost center — in your accounting software, in your chart of accounts, or with your bank — specifically for that award.

Every expense charged to a federal award must be supported by documentation: invoices, receipts, timesheets, contracts with vendors, or other records that prove the expense was incurred and that it was allowable, allocable, and reasonable under the terms of your award. Keep these records organized and accessible. Federal awards can be audited for up to three years after the close-out of the award period, which means you need to retain documentation long after the work is done.

Most grants require a final financial report to be submitted within 60 to 90 days of the end of the period of performance. This report accounts for every dollar received and every dollar spent. Any unspent funds at the end of the award period are typically returned to the agency, unless you have received written approval to carry them forward. Know your close-out deadlines and plan for them in advance.

If your organization has not previously managed federal awards, strongly consider engaging a certified public accountant who is familiar with OMB Uniform Guidance — the federal regulations governing grant financial management — before your first award arrives. The investment in qualified guidance at the beginning of a federal funding relationship is significantly less expensive than the cost of a compliance finding later.

Audit Readiness — What It Means and How to Prepare

Any organization that expends $750,000 or more in federal awards in a single fiscal year is required to have a Single Audit — a specialized financial audit conducted under the requirements of the

Uniform Guidance. If your organization is new to federal funding, you may be well below that threshold for several years. But audit readiness is not only about the Single Audit threshold. It is about maintaining the discipline that allows you to demonstrate accountability at any point during your award period.

Audit readiness means three things practically. First, your financial records are organized and complete, and they can produce documentation to support any expenditure charged to a federal award. Second, your organization has documented internal controls — written policies for how federal funds are approved, spent, and reported — that demonstrate you have a system in place, not just individuals making judgment calls. Third, your board is engaged and informed about the organization's federal compliance obligations, and minutes reflect that oversight.

The APEX Accelerator network — the same free resource mentioned in the previous chapter for Sources Sought support — also provides assistance with financial readiness and compliance preparation. If you are approaching your first award and are uncertain about your financial systems, reach out to your nearest APEX Accelerator before the award arrives. That conversation will cost you nothing and could prevent a compliance finding that costs considerably more.

Your Compliance Calendar

The table below covers all recurring obligations that belong on your compliance calendar from the moment you receive an award. Build this structure before you need it — so when the award arrives, you are tracking, not catching up.

Compliance Item	Frequency	When to Act
SAM.gov registration renewal	Annual	Set a reminder 60 days before expiration
Performance progress report	Quarterly or semi-annual	Per award terms — mark all deadlines on the day of the award
Financial expenditure report	Quarterly, monthly, or at close-out	Per award terms — confirm with grants officer
Final financial report	Once, at close-out	Due 60–90 days after the period of performance ends
Certification renewals (WOSB, HUBZone, etc.)	Annual or biennial	Set a reminder 90 days before each expiration
Sub-award reporting (if applicable)	As incurred	Within 30 days of executing any qualifying subcontract
Single Audit (if $750K+ in federal awards)	Annual	Engage CPA no later than 60 days after the fiscal year-end

What to Do If Something Goes Wrong

Problems happen — programs run behind schedule, budgets need adjustments, staff turnover occurs, and emergencies arise. The worst thing you can do when something goes wrong on a federal award is to stay quiet and hope it resolves itself. The best thing you can do is contact your contracting officer or grants officer immediately, before the problem compounds.

Federal agencies are not looking for reasons to terminate awards. Most agencies will work with you on modifications, no-cost extensions, budget adjustments, or corrective action plans — if you communicate proactively and professionally. What agencies cannot work with is silence, missed reports, and surprises at the close-out review. The contracting officer is your partner in this process. Treat them as one.

Document everything. Every phone call about a problem, every email exchange, every decision made — keep a written record with dates and names. If the agency approves a modification verbally, follow up with a written confirmation email. If you implement a corrective action, document what you did and when. This record serves as your protection if questions arise later and demonstrates the kind of professional accountability that builds long-term agency relationships.

Pro Tip

Create your Compliance Calendar the day you receive your award notice — not the week your first report is due. Mark every deadline from the award document: quarterly reporting dates, financial report dates, your SAM.gov renewal, your certification renewals, and the period of performance end date. Review it on the first Monday of every month. The organizations that remain in good standing are the ones that treat compliance as a system, not a reaction.

Real Talk

Compliance is not the most exciting part of federal contracting. It is, however, the part that determines whether you get to do it again. One missed report, one lapsed registration, one commingled bank account — these are the things that close doors that took years to open. Build the habits now, before the award arrives, and compliance becomes routine rather than a crisis.

Closing Action

Build your Compliance Calendar template today — before your first award arrives. Create a document or spreadsheet with these columns: Award Name, Reporting Type, Deadline, Responsible Person, and Status. Add your SAM.gov renewal date and any active certification renewal dates right now. When your first federal award comes in, you will have a system ready to receive it.

Systems and compliance keep you in good standing. Relationships keep you competitive. Chapter 12 shows you how to build the government relationships that influence which opportunities get set aside, how solicitations get written, and who gets the call when a contracting officer has a question — and why the relationship skills you have spent your entire ministry career developing are exactly the ones the federal marketplace rewards.

— End of Chapter 11 —

PART FOUR | THE PIPELINE

CHAPTER TWELVE

Building Relationships with Government Agencies

"How do I build relationships with the right people?"

Here is something the federal contracting world rarely advertises: the technical proposal is not always the deciding factor. Relationships shape which opportunities get set aside for specific categories of vendors. Relationships influence how solicitations are written — what language is used, which certifications are preferred, and what past performance looks like. Relationships determine who the contracting officer calls when they have a quick question before the award decision. And relationships are why some organizations keep winning, while others keep submitting proposals that never get selected.

Diana already knows how to build trust. She has been doing it her entire career — with families in crisis, with community partners, with elected officials, with donors who gave because they believed in her and her team. The skills that built those relationships are exactly the skills that build federal ones. This chapter shows her where to apply them.

The Agency Small Business Office — Your Most Important Contact

Every federal agency with significant contracting activity must have a Small Business Office. The staff in that office — typically Small Business Specialists or Small Business Representatives — exist specifically to help organizations like yours access federal contracting opportunities. Their job is to advocate for small-business participation within their agency, to connect qualified vendors with the appropriate procurement offices, and to help contracting officers identify set-aside candidates for upcoming solicitations.

This is not a cold call. It is an introduction to someone whose job description includes meeting you. Search for '[Agency name] small business office' or navigate to the procurement or business opportunities section of the agency's website. Most agencies publish their Small Business Office contact information publicly. When you find it, send a brief, professional introduction email — attach your capability statement, name your primary NAICS codes and certifications, and request a thirty-minute introduction call. Keep the ask simple and specific. A thirty-minute call. That is the standard entry point, and it is rarely refused.

Come to that call prepared. Know the agency's mission. Know which of their program areas align with your organization's capabilities. Have two or three past performance examples ready to describe. Ask about upcoming opportunities that align with your service area and whether there are industry days or pre-solicitation events you should attend. Then follow up with a thank-you email within 24 hours, attaching your capability statement. That follow-up is the beginning of the relationship log you will maintain from this point forward.

OSDBU — The Office That Advocates for You

The Office of Small and Disadvantaged Business Utilization — OSDBU — is the advocacy office within each federal agency for small, minority-owned, women-owned, and veteran-owned businesses and nonprofits. OSDBU offices are distinct from the Small Business Office in that they carry explicit advocacy authority — they exist not just to connect vendors with opportunities, but to ensure that agencies are actively meeting their small business utilization goals.

There is no single central directory for all federal OSDBU offices, but most agencies make theirs easy to find. The majority follow a consistent URL pattern — go to the agency's main website and append '/osdbu' (for example, va.gov/osdbu, usda.gov/osdbu, hhs.gov/osdbu). For agencies that don't follow that pattern, search '[Agency name] Office of Small and Disadvantaged Business Utilization' and their page will surface directly. OSDBU offices can connect you directly with contracting opportunities, introduce you to program officers in relevant divisions, and advocate for set-aside decisions that benefit certified vendors like you.

When you reach out to an OSDBU office, introduce yourself clearly: your organization's name, your certifications, your primary service areas, and the types of opportunities you are pursuing. Share your capability statement. Ask what programs within their agency fund work in your area, and ask to be informed of upcoming industry days or matchmaking events. A relationship with an OSDBU office is one of the most direct pathways from introduction to opportunity in the federal system.

Who to Contact and How

Contact	Their Role	How to Reach Them
Small Business Specialist	Connects vendors to agency contract opportunities; advises on set-aside decisions	Agency website — search '[Agency] small business office'
OSDBU Director	Advocates for small, women-owned, veteran-owned, and disadvantaged business participation	Agency website — search '[Agency name] OSDBU' or go to [agency].gov/osdbu
Contracting Officer	Issues solicitations and awards contracts; manages the procurement process	Listed on SAM.gov solicitations and Sources Sought notices
Program Officer / Manager	Manages the funded program and works with award recipients on performance	Identified in grant award documents; attend agency industry days
APEX Accelerator Counselor	Free technical assistance for small businesses and nonprofits pursuing federal contracts	apexaccelerators.us — find your nearest location

How to Request a Capability Briefing

A capability briefing is a short meeting — typically fifteen to thirty minutes — in which you present your organization's capabilities directly to an agency representative. It is one of the most effective relationship-building tools available to a small business or nonprofit in the federal marketplace, and it is completely standard practice. Agencies expect these requests. Contracting officers and small business specialists hold them regularly.

Request a capability briefing by email to the contracting officer or small business specialist at your target agency. Keep the email brief — three short paragraphs are enough. Introduce yourself and your organization, list your certifications and primary NAICS codes, reference one or two past performance highlights, and request a 15- to 30-minute call or meeting at their convenience. Attach your capability statement. A useful subject line format: 'Capability Briefing Request — [Organization Name] — NAICS [Code] — [Certification(s)].'

In the briefing itself, lead with the agency's mission — not your organization's story. Show that you understand what the agency is trying to accomplish and then explain specifically how your capabilities serve that mission. Bring data: numbers of people served, outcomes achieved, partners engaged. Ask questions. What program areas are they planning to expand? What types of vendors are they looking for? What upcoming opportunities might be a fit? Close by asking to be notified of relevant solicitations and thanking them for their time. Then send a follow-up email within twenty-four hours.

Industry Days and Pre-Solicitation Events

Industry days are agency-hosted events where upcoming procurement opportunities are announced, program requirements are outlined, and vendors can ask questions and meet agency staff. Attending an industry day on an opportunity relevant to your mission is one of the highest-return activities available to a faith-based organization entering the federal marketplace. You are in the same room as the contracting officer, the program manager, and every other potential competitor — and you have the chance to make a human impression before a single proposal has been written.

Pre-solicitation conferences serve a similar purpose but are held specifically before a formal solicitation is released. Agencies use them to gather vendor input on the requirements, clarify scope questions, and hear from the market before the contract terms are finalized. Your questions at a pre-solicitation conference can actually influence how the solicitation is written — which means organizations that attend are shaping the terms of the competition before it begins.

Bring printed copies of your capability statement to every industry day and matchmaking event — twenty to thirty copies minimum. Introduce yourself to agency staff by name. Collect business cards and contact information. And follow up within forty-eight hours with a brief email referencing your conversation. That follow-up is what separates an attendee from a contact.

The Faith-Based Advantage in Relationship Building

Federal program officers and contracting officers who manage community-serving programs — housing, workforce development, food security, veteran services, behavioral health — are often frustrated by one persistent gap: organizations with the deepest community relationships rarely appear in the federal marketplace. The organizations that do show up sometimes lack the embedded trust, the volunteer infrastructure, and the genuine community presence that make program delivery effective.

Your faith-based organization has what they cannot manufacture. Decades of relationship history in a specific neighborhood. A network of volunteers who extend your reach without extending your budget. A name that families recognize and trust when they walk through your doors. Community partners — schools, hospitals, housing authorities, law enforcement — who already know your work. These are not soft differentiators. They are genuine competitive advantages in programs where community trust is the difference between a service that reaches people and one that doesn't.

Name these advantages plainly in your capability briefings, your capability statement, and your agency conversations. Do not bury your community embeddedness in ministry language. Translate it: 'twenty-two years of embedded service relationships in [community], a volunteer network of 140 active community members, existing partnerships with [county health department, local school district, housing authority].' That is a differentiator that a program officer can act on.

And do not hide your faith identity. The federal equal treatment policy means your faith framework is not a liability. For agencies looking to fund community-based service delivery, it is often an asset — a signal that your organization's roots go deeper than a grant cycle and that your commitment to the community does not end when the funding period does.

Pro Tip

After every agency interaction — a capability briefing, an industry day, a Sources Sought response — send a follow-up email within 48 hours. Reference something specific from the conversation. Attach your capability statement if you haven't already. Ask to be added to their notification list for relevant opportunities. One sentence, one attachment, one ask. That habit, repeated consistently, builds the recognition that turns introductions into awards.

Real Talk

You are not asking for a favor. You are introducing a qualified organization that can help a federal agency achieve its mission. The government needs vendors who can deliver community-based services with credibility, reach, and accountability. You are one. Walk into every agency meeting with that understanding — and let it show.

Closing Action

Identify two or three federal agencies that fund work relevant to your ministry's primary service area. Find the Small Business Office or OSDBU contact for each one — use agency websites and osdbu.gov. Draft one capability briefing request email this week using the subject line format in this chapter. Attach your capability statement. Send it. Log the outreach in your Opportunity Calendar with the date, contact name, and agency.

You have the tools, registrations, certifications, capability statement, search system, and relationships. Everything you have built across this book comes together in Chapter 13, which shows you how to turn a single award into a sustainable pipeline that funds your ministry's mission not just this year, but for years to come.

— End of Chapter 12 —

PART FOUR | THE PIPELINE

CHAPTER THIRTEEN

From First Award to Sustainable Pipeline

"How do I turn this into something that actually lasts?"

One contract does not make a strategy. One grant does not make a ministry sustainable. What transforms this work from a series of applications into a genuine funding pipeline is intention — the decision to treat the federal marketplace not as a one-time opportunity but as a long-term relationship worth investing in.

Diana came into this book with a question. She leaves with a system, a credential, a document, a search strategy, and a clearer picture of the landscape than most organizations twice her size. What she builds from here depends on what she does in the next twelve months. This chapter gives her the framework to do it with purpose.

Lessons from Your First Award — What to Document

Your first federal award is not just a contract or a grant — it is your most important piece of competitive intelligence. The organizations that grow consistently in the federal marketplace are the ones that treat every award as a learning document, not just a funding source.

From the moment your first award becomes active, begin recording your observations. What aspects of program delivery went smoothly? What took longer than you planned? What did the agency ask for in reporting that you had not anticipated? What would you do differently in the proposal if you were writing it today? These are not abstract reflections — they are the inputs that make your next proposal stronger, your next report cleaner, and your next award conversation more confident.

At closeout, request a past-performance evaluation from your contracting officer or grants officer. This is a formal document that federal agencies use to assess prior award recipients when making future award decisions. Not every agency provides them automatically, but most will provide one if you ask. Keep it on file. Keep the contact information of the program officer and contracting officer current. These are references — and federal agencies do call them.

Your first award is also the foundation of your past performance record. Before this award, you had a community history. After it, you have federal history. That distinction matters enormously in the competitive evaluation of future proposals. The path from the first award to the second award runs directly through the documentation you maintain on the first one.

Building Your Past Performance Record Over Time

Past performance is cumulative. Every award you complete, every report you submit on time, every close-out you handle cleanly adds to a record that federal agencies can access and verify. Organizations that have been in the federal marketplace for five years with a clean past performance record have a structural advantage over new entrants — but that record had to start somewhere. Yours starts with your first award.

Maintain a Past Performance folder — physical or digital — that captures key information for every program you have delivered, federal or otherwise. For each program, record the name and description, the funding source or awarding agency, the period of performance, the total dollar value, the number of people served, the outcomes achieved, and the name and contact information of the government or organizational point of contact. Update it every time a program closes.

Do not limit your past performance folder to federal awards. Significant community programs funded through state agencies, local governments, private foundations, or major institutional partners are relevant past performance — especially in the early years before your federal record is established. A three-year food security program funded through the county, serving 1,200 people annually, is a past performance. Write it up and keep it ready.

Teaming and Subcontracting as a Growth Strategy

Not every path into federal contracting runs through a prime award. For many faith-based organizations, the most practical entry point is as a subcontractor — a community-based partner that a larger prime contractor brings in to deliver specific program components in a specific geographic area. This strategy lets you build federal experience, earn past performance, and develop agency relationships without competing head-to-head against organizations with years of federal contracting history.

Teaming is a related strategy where two or more organizations formally partner to pursue a contract together, combining their capabilities, certifications, and past performance into a single bid. If you bring the community presence, the volunteer infrastructure, and the certified status, and your teaming partner brings the contracting history and the administrative systems, together, you may be more competitive than either organization would be on its own.

To find teaming partners, start with the APEX Accelerator network — counselors can connect you with other small businesses and nonprofits in your area who are pursuing similar opportunities. Industry days and matchmaking events are also productive teaming grounds — you are in the same room as organizations working in the same space, and a conversation at an industry day has launched more than a few lasting teaming relationships. The SAM.gov Dynamic Small Business Search is a public database where you can search for certified small businesses by NAICS code and location — use it to identify potential partners who are already registered and active in your program area.

Your 12-Month Pipeline Planning Framework

The table below provides a starting framework for your first 12 months in the federal marketplace. Adapt it to your organization's current position — if you are already registered and certified, you may be starting at Quarter 2. If you are building from scratch, Quarter 1 is your foundation. Either way, the framework is a working document, not a rigid schedule. Update it as your situation develops.

Timeline	Focus	Key Actions
Quarter 1	**Foundation**	Complete SAM.gov registration, certifications, and capability

Timeline	Focus	Key Actions
		statement. Set up saved searches and email alerts. Begin keyword library.
Quarters 1-2	**Market Entry**	Respond to 2-3 Sources Sought notices. Attend 1-2 industry days. Make 3 agency contacts. Begin compliance calendar.
Quarters 2-3	**First Submission**	Submit the first grant application. Explore teaming opportunities. Build financial tracking infrastructure for the anticipated award.
Quarters 3-4	**Refine and Expand**	Evaluate first submissions. Refine the capability statement. Expand NAICS codes if new programs have been launched. Deepen 1-2 agency relationships.
Year 2	**Grow the Pipeline**	Pursue the first contract solicitation. Add a second funding stream. Build subcontracting relationships. Close out or manage an active award.
Year 3+	**Sustainable Pipeline**	Multiple active awards. Regular agency relationships. Established a past performance record. Mentoring newer entrants.

When to Bring in Help

You do not have to do all of this alone — and at certain stages, trying to do so will cost you more than the help would. Knowing when to bring in specialized support is not a sign of limitation. It is a sign of strategy.

Grant writers are most valuable when you are pursuing a competitive grant that requires a long, structured narrative proposal — the kind where the quality of the writing directly affects your score. Not every grant requires a professional writer; many shorter applications can be handled in-house with strong organizational leadership. But when a major competitive grant represents a significant funding opportunity, and the application is dense, a grant writer who knows the program area is an investment worth making.

Compliance consultants become valuable before your first audit or when you are managing multiple federal awards simultaneously. If your financial systems are not set up for federal cost accounting, a consultant familiar with OMB Uniform Guidance can save you from findings that are far more expensive than the consulting fee.

The APEX Accelerator remains your highest-value resource throughout this entire journey because it is free. APEX counselors provide one-on-one guidance, proposal review, compliance preparation, teaming connections, and training at no cost to qualifying small businesses and nonprofits. Find your nearest APEX Accelerator at apexaccelerators.us. If you have not connected with one yet, do it this week.

Keeping Mission Central as You Scale

The federal marketplace is a powerful funding tool. It is not, however, a neutral one. As you pursue federal opportunities, you will encounter programs that partially fit your mission — close enough that the funding is tempting, but not quite aligned with the community you were called to serve or the way you were called to serve them. You will encounter reporting requirements that push you toward measuring what is easy to count rather than what actually matters. You will encounter growth pressures that can shift your organization's focus from the community toward the contract.

None of this is insurmountable. But all of it requires intentional leadership. Federal funding is a resource for your mission — it is not the mission itself. The organizations that sustain themselves the longest in this marketplace are the ones that maintain clarity about why they entered it in the first place and regularly return to that question as they grow.

As you scale, build in regular moments of mission alignment — board conversations, staff retreats, community listening sessions — where you ask plainly: Is what we are pursuing still aligned with who we were called to serve? The answer may always be yes. But the discipline of asking keeps you anchored to the reason you showed up in the first place.

Diana did not leave the ministry to become a contractor. She became a contractor to sustain her ministry. Every federal dollar she earns goes back into the community she was called to serve. That is the vision. Keep it in front of you — at every industry day, in every proposal, and in every award letter you sign.

Real Talk

You did not leave the ministry to become a contractor. You became a contractor to sustain your ministry. Every federal dollar you earn is a dollar that goes back into the community you were called to serve. That is the vision. Keep it in front of you — at every industry day, in every proposal, and in every award letter you open.

Resource
The APEX Accelerator program (apexaccelerators.us) offers free, one-on-one counseling, proposal reviews, and training for organizations at every stage of the federal contracting journey. Every state has at least one location. If you have been doing this alone, you do not have to anymore.

Closing Action
Write your 12-month pipeline plan. Use the Quarter 1 through Year 2 framework in this chapter as your starting template. Fill in your specific programs, your target agencies, and your certification goals. Identify the one action you can take this week — and take it. This is not a wish list. It is a working document. Date it, revisit it monthly, and update it as you move.

You have been called. You have been equipped. Now go get contracted.

— End of Chapter 15 —

GLOSSARY

Federal Contracting Terms for Faith-Based Organizations

The terms below appear throughout this book. Use this glossary as a quick reference whenever an unfamiliar term surfaces in a solicitation, a portal, or an agency conversation.

Term	Definition
8(a) Program	The SBA program provides contracting advantages to small businesses owned by socially and economically disadvantaged individuals. Participants can receive sole-source awards up to $4.5M for services.
ALN (Assistance Listing Number)	Formerly called the CFDA number. A unique five-digit identifier is assigned to every federal assistance program. Use it to search for current and past grant opportunities on Grants.gov.
APEX Accelerator	Free federal contracting technical assistance program (formerly Procurement Technical Assistance Centers). Provides proposal review, compliance guidance, and one-on-one counseling.
CAGE Code	Commercial and Government Entity code — a five-character identifier assigned to your organization after SAM.gov

Term	Definition
	registration and required on capability statements and federal submissions.
Capability Statement	A one-page document introducing your organization to federal contracting officers and prime contractors. Includes core competencies, past performance, differentiators, company data, and contact information.
CFDA Number	See ALN (Assistance Listing Number). Legacy term still used in some contexts.
Contracting Officer (CO)	The federal employee has the legal authority to enter into, administer, and terminate contracts on behalf of the government. Your primary point of contact for contract-related matters.
Cooperative Agreement	A federal award similar to a grant, but with substantial agency involvement in the program's implementation. Falls between a grant and a contract in terms of agency engagement.
EDWOSB	Economically Disadvantaged Women-Owned Small Business. An additional SBA certification for WOSB-eligible organizations whose qualifying women meet specific income and asset thresholds.
Entity	The term SAM.gov uses for a registered organization. Your SAM.gov 'entity' is your organization's federal identity.

Term	Definition
Grants.gov	The federal government's centralized portal for all competitive grant and cooperative agreement opportunities. Required search point for federal grant funding.
HUBZone	Historically Underutilized Business Zone. An SBA certification for organizations located in economically distressed areas. Provides set-aside access and a 10% price evaluation preference.
Industry Day	An agency-hosted event announcing upcoming procurement opportunities and allowing vendors to meet agency staff and ask questions before a solicitation is released.
NAICS Code	North American Industry Classification System code. A six-digit code classifying your organization's service area. Determines which opportunities you appear in when agencies search for vendors.
OSDBU	Office of Small and Disadvantaged Business Utilization. An advocacy office within each federal agency supporting small, women-owned, veteran-owned, and disadvantaged business participation.
Past Performance	A record of prior work delivered — federal or otherwise — is used to demonstrate capability in future proposals. Includes program description, funder,

Term	Definition
	outcomes, dollar value, and reference contacts.
Period of Performance	The official start and end dates during which a federal award is active, and deliverables must be completed.
Pre-Solicitation Notice	An early announcement on SAM.gov that a solicitation is forthcoming. Provides advance warning to begin preparation before the formal opportunity is posted.
Prime Contractor	An organization that holds a direct federal contract and may engage subcontractors to deliver portions of the work.
RFP (Request for Proposal)	A formal solicitation document inviting organizations to submit competitive proposals for a federal contract. Includes evaluation criteria, scope of work, and submission requirements.
SAM.gov	System for Award Management. The federal government's primary portal for registration and contracting opportunities. Required for all federal contract and grant recipients.
SDVOSB	Service-Disabled Veteran-Owned Small Business. An SBA certification for businesses owned and controlled by veterans with a service-connected disability rating.

Term	Definition
Set-Aside	A contract or grant competition restricted to a specific category of vendor — such as small businesses, WOSB-certified, or HUBZone-certified organizations.
Single Audit	A specialized financial audit is required for organizations expending $750,000 or more in federal awards in a fiscal year, conducted under OMB Uniform Guidance requirements.
Small Business Office	An office within each federal agency connecting small businesses to contracting opportunities and advising on set-aside decisions.
Sources Sought Notice	A market research notice posted on SAM.gov asks vendors to identify themselves before a solicitation is written. Responding is low-risk and high-value for relationship building.
Subcontractor	An organization engaged by a prime contractor to deliver a portion of a federal contract. Subcontracting is a common entry point for new federal market participants.
UEI (Unique Entity Identifier)	A 12-character alphanumeric identifier assigned to every organization registered in SAM.gov. Replaced the DUNS number in 2022. Required on all federal submissions.
Uniform Guidance	OMB's regulations (2 CFR Part 200) govern the financial management, audit

Term	Definition
	requirements, and cost principles for federal grant recipients.
USASpending.gov	The federal government's public spending database. Shows all federal awards — who received them, from which agency, under which program, and for what amount.
VOSB	Veteran-Owned Small Business. An SBA certification for businesses at least 51% owned and controlled by one or more veterans.
WOSB	Women-Owned Small Business. An SBA certification for businesses at least 51% owned and controlled by women who are US citizens. Qualifies the organization for WOSB set-aside contracts.

APPENDIX A

Federal Agency Quick Reference

The agencies below are among the most active funders of community-based, faith-adjacent, and social services work. Use this table to identify your target agencies, find their opportunity portals, and connect with the right office within each one.

Agency	What They Fund	Where to Search	Key Contact
HUD	Housing, homelessness, community development, veteran housing	hudexchange.info	Agency Small Business Office or OSDBU
HHS	Mental health, substance use, social services, and community health	hhs.gov/grants	Office of Small and Disadvantaged Business Utilization
DOL	Workforce development, veteran employment, and job training	dol.gov/agencies/eta/ grants	Office of Small and Disadvantaged Business Utilization
FEMA	Emergency food and shelter,	fema.gov/grants	FEMA Non-Disaster

Agency	What They Fund	Where to Search	Key Contact
	disaster relief, community resilience		Grants Division
USDA	Rural development, food and nutrition programs, community facilities	usda.gov/topics/farming/ grants-and-loans	Office of Small and Disadvantaged Business Utilization
VA	Veteran services, homeless veteran housing, and employment reintegration	va.gov/osdbu	VA OSDBU — veteran-focused community partners
DOJ	Reentry services, crime victim assistance, community safety	justice.gov/grants	Office of Small and Disadvantaged Business Utilization
SBA	Small business development, certifications, and technical assistance	sba.gov	Local SBA district office or SCORE chapter
DHS	Community resilience,	dhs.gov/grants	Office of Small and

Agency	What They Fund	Where to Search	Key Contact
	emergency preparedness, and trafficking prevention		Disadvantaged Business Utilization

APPENDIX B

Pre-Registration Checklist

Complete every item on this checklist before beginning your SAM.gov registration. Missing any of these items mid-registration will pause the process and may add days or weeks to your timeline. Check off each item as it is confirmed.

	Item	Notes / Where to Get It
☐	**Legal Organization Name**	Must match exactly across all federal documents — IRS, state filings, and SAM.gov.
☐	**Employer Identification Number (EIN)**	Assigned by the IRS. Required for SAM.gov registration. Apply at irs.gov if you don't have one.
☐	**Legal Business Address**	Physical address of your principal office. P.O. boxes are not accepted as the primary address.
☐	**Articles of Incorporation or Organization**	Proof of your legal formation filed with your state.
☐	**501(c)(3) Determination Letter**	IRS letter confirming nonprofit status. Required for faith-based nonprofits applying for grants.

	Item	Notes / Where to Get It
☐	**DUNS Number / UEI**	A UEI (Unique Entity Identifier) is now assigned during SAM.gov registration. No pre-registration step needed.
☐	**Login.gov Account**	Required to access SAM.gov. Create at login.gov before starting registration.
☐	**Banking Information**	Routing number and account number for the bank account that will receive federal payments.
☐	**Primary NAICS Code(s) Identified**	Review the NAICS code table in Chapter 5 and identify your primary and secondary codes before registering.
☐	**Fiscal Year End Date**	The date your organization's fiscal year ends (e.g., December 31 or June 30).
☐	**Authorized Organization Representative (AOR)**	The person with legal authority to register and certify the organization in SAM.gov.
☐	**Point of Contact for Federal Inquiries**	Name, title, phone, and email of the person who handles federal contracting or grant inquiries.

APPENDIX C

Capability Statement Template

This template covers all six required elements of a federal capability statement. Fill in your organization's specific information in each section. The completed document should fit on one page when formatted with your organization's branding.

[ORGANIZATION NAME]

[Tagline or mission statement — one sentence]

CORE COMPETENCIES

• [Service area 1 — use federal search language]

• [Service area 2]

• [Service area 3]

• [Service area 4]

• [Service area 5]

PAST PERFORMANCE

[Program Name] — [Funding source/partner agency]. [Scope of work, population served.] [Measurable outcome — number served, timeframe, results.]

[Program Name] — [Funding source/partner agency]. [Scope of work, population served.] [Measurable outcome.]

[Program Name] — [Funding source/partner agency]. [Scope of work, population served.] [Measurable outcome.]

DIFFERENTIATORS

• [Years of embedded community service in (geographic area)]

• [Faith-based organization with existing community trust and volunteer infrastructure]

• [Active certifications — WOSB, HUBZone, SDVOSB, etc.]

• [Key partnerships — county agencies, school districts, hospitals, etc.]

COMPANY DATA

UEI: _______________ | CAGE Code: _______________ | Entity Type: Nonprofit / Faith-Based Organization

Primary NAICS: _______________ | Secondary NAICS: _______________, _______________

Certifications: _______________ | Year Established: _______________

CONTACT

[Name], [Title] | [Phone] | [Email] | [Website]

APPENDIX D

Opportunity Evaluation Worksheet

Use this worksheet before committing time and resources to any federal opportunity. If any answer is No, move on without guilt. If all answers are Yes, add the opportunity to your calendar and begin preparation.

Evaluation Question	Yes	No	Notes
Do we actually provide this type of service?	☐	☐	
Are we eligible to apply (size, certification, nonprofit status)?	☐	☐	
Can we realistically meet the application deadline?	☐	☐	
Do we have the staff capacity to deliver if awarded?	☐	☐	
Is the award size proportional to the effort required to apply?	☐	☐	

Opportunity Name:

Issuing Agency:

Deadline:

Award Amount / Range:

NAICS Code or ALN:

Set-Aside Type (if applicable):

Decision (Pursue / Pass):

Next Action Step:

APPENDIX E

Sources Sought Response Template

Use this template to respond to any Sources Sought notice posted on SAM.gov. Replace all bracketed fields with your organization's specific information and the agency's specific questions. Attach your capability statement to every response.

SOURCES SOUGHT RESPONSE

Notice Number: [Copy from SAM.gov posting]
Agency: [Issuing agency name]
Date Submitted: [Date]

ORGANIZATION INFORMATION

Organization Name: [Legal name as registered in SAM.gov]
UEI: [Your UEI] | CAGE Code: [Your CAGE code]
Primary NAICS: [Code] | Certifications: [List all active certifications]

INTRODUCTION

[Organization Name] is a [nonprofit/faith-based organization] with [X years] of experience providing [core service area] to [target population] in [geographic area]. We hold [list certifications] and are actively registered in SAM.gov under UEI [number]. We respectfully submit this response to the Sources Sought notice referenced above.

RESPONSE TO AGENCY QUESTIONS

Question 1: [Copy the agency's exact question]
Response: [Your direct, specific answer]

Question 2: [Copy the agency's exact question]
Response: [Your direct, specific answer]

PAST PERFORMANCE

Example 1: [Program name] — [Funding source or partner agency]. [Scope of work and population served.] [Measurable outcome — number served, timeframe, results.]

Example 2: [Program name] — [Funding source or partner agency]. [Scope of work and population served.] [Measurable outcome.]

CLOSING

[Organization Name] is highly interested in the anticipated solicitation resulting from this Sources Sought. We respectfully request notification when the solicitation is posted. Our capability statement is attached for your reference. For questions, please contact [Name], [Title], at [Phone] or [Email].

APPENDIX F

Compliance Calendar Template

Complete this calendar on the day you receive each federal award. Review it on the first Monday of every month. Add rows for each additional award you receive.

Award Name / Program	Award Amount	Reporting Deadline	Financial Deadline	Status

Annual Renewal Item	Expiration Date	Reminder Set (60 Days Prior)
SAM.gov Registration		☐

Annual Renewal Item	Expiration Date	Reminder Set (60 Days Prior)
WOSB / EDWOSB Certification		☐
HUBZone Certification		☐
VOSB / SDVOSB Certification		☐
8(a) Program Status		☐

APPENDIX G

12-Month Pipeline Planning Worksheet

Use this worksheet to map your federal market entry plan. Fill in specific programs, agencies, deadlines, and goals for each phase. Update it monthly as your situation develops. Date it so you can track your progress over time.

Planning Start Date: ______________________

Organization Name: ______________________

Phase	Focus	My Specific Goals and Actions
Quarter 1	**Foundation**	SAM.gov registration complete by: ___ Certifications to pursue: ___ Capability statement drafted by: ___ Saved searches set up: ___
Quarters 1-2	**Market Entry**	Sources Sought responses to submit: ___ Industry days to attend: ___ Agency contacts to make: ___
Quarters 2-3	**First Submission**	Grant application target: ___ Agency: ___ Deadline: ___ Teaming partners to identify: ___
Quarters	**Refine**	Capability statement update date: ___

Phase	Focus	My Specific Goals and Actions
3-4		New NAICS codes to add: ___ Agency relationships to deepen: ___
Year 2	Grow	First contract solicitation target: ___ Second funding stream: ___ Subcontracting opportunities: ___

FEDERAL RESOURCES

Organized by Topic

All resources below are publicly available and free to access. Bookmark the ones most relevant to your current stage and revisit this section as you grow.

FEDERAL PORTALS

Resource	Website	What It Does for You
SAM.gov	**sam.gov**	Register your entity, search contract opportunities, manage certifications, and maintain your federal profile.
Grants.gov	**grants.gov**	Search for and apply for all federal competitive grants and cooperative agreements across all agencies.
USASpending.gov	**usaspending.gov**	Research who is already receiving federal funding, which agencies fund your mission area, and who your potential teaming partners are.
beta.SAM.gov	**sam.gov**	The current SAM.gov interface — use this for all

Resource	Website	What It Does for You
		searches and registration activities.

CERTIFICATIONS

Certification	Website	Notes
WOSB / EDWOSB / HUBZone / 8(a)	**certify.sba.gov**	SBA's certification portal for all four major small business certifications. Create an account and apply directly.
VOSB / SDVOSB	**vetbiz.va.gov**	VA's veteran small business certification portal. Required for formal VOSB and SDVOSB designation.
SBA Size Standards	**sba.gov/size-standards**	Confirm your organization meets the size standard for your primary NAICS code before applying for any SBA certification.

TECHNICAL ASSISTANCE

Resource	Website	What They Offer
APEX Accelerators	**apexaccelerators.us**	Free one-on-one counseling, proposal review, compliance guidance, and training for small businesses and nonprofits at every stage.
SBA Learning Center	**sba.gov/learning-center**	Free online courses covering federal contracting basics, certification programs, and business development.
SCORE	**score.org**	Free mentoring from experienced business professionals. Useful for organizational development and business planning.

NAICS AND CLASSIFICATION

Resource	Website	What It Does for You
NAICS Association	**naics.com**	Search for NAICS codes by keyword. Find the right codes for your programs before registering in SAM.gov.

Resource	Website	What It Does for You
Census Bureau NAICS	**census.gov/naics**	The authoritative source for NAICS code definitions. Read full definitions — not just titles — to confirm a code applies to your work.
SAM.gov Assistance Listings	**sam.gov/assistance-listings**	Search every federal assistance program by ALN, keyword, or agency—the master database of all grant programs.

KEY AGENCY RESOURCES

Agency / Program	Website	Notes
HUD Exchange	**hudexchange.info**	HUD's grant program resource hub. Find Continuum of Care, ESG, HOPWA, HOME, and other community-serving programs.
HHS Grants	**hhs.gov/grants**	Health and Human Services grant opportunities, including mental health, substance use, and social services programs.

Agency / Program	Website	Notes
DOL Grants	**dol.gov/**	Department of Labor grant programs, including HVRP (veteran reintegration) and workforce development funding.
VA OSDBU	**va.gov/osdbu**	VA's Office of Small and Disadvantaged Business Utilization. Key contact for veteran-serving organizations.
FEMA Grants	**fema.gov/grants**	FEMA non-disaster grant programs, including Emergency Food and Shelter and community resilience funding.

ABOUT THE PUBLISHER

Pen 2 Paper Publishers is a publishing house dedicated to equipping faith-based organizations, small businesses, ministry leaders, and community-driven nonprofits with practical, accessible resources for navigating the federal marketplace. With a deep understanding of both the calling that drives ministry leaders into service and the systems that govern federal funding, Pen 2 Paper Publishers bridges the gap between mission and marketplace.

Called and Contracted was written out of a conviction that the organizations most trusted by vulnerable communities — the ones with the deepest roots, the longest track records, and the most genuine relationships — are often the least represented in federal procurement. This book was written for the leader who has spent years serving without funding that matches the mission, and who is finally ready to change that.

Through its publications, Pen 2 Paper Publishers helps faith-based leaders and small business owners translate their experience and community impact into the credentials the federal government recognizes and rewards — equipping organizations to pursue contracts, grants, and federal partnerships with confidence, clarity, and purpose.

Pen 2 Paper Publishers

pen2paperpublishers.com

ABOUT THE AUTHOR

LaSonya DeBose spent eleven years in ministry before she ever opened a federal portal. What she found on the other side changed the trajectory of her work — and became the foundation for everything she now teaches. She understood firsthand what it meant to lead a faith community with limited resources and unlimited vision, and she refused to accept that the two could not be reconciled. That refusal became a calling of a different kind.

Today, LaSonya is a government contracting strategist and compliance specialist based in North Carolina. As the founder of Pen 2 Paper Consulting and Pen 2 Paper Publishers, and a certified Woman-Owned Small Business (WOSB/EDWOSB), her work spans government contracting, business consulting, and publishing. Her expertise in SAM.gov registration and federal procurement has made her a trusted resource for small business owners and faith-based organizations navigating the government marketplace — translating complex federal systems into clear, actionable steps for leaders who are ready to compete.

Called and Contracted was created to help the organizations most trusted by vulnerable communities gain access to the federal resources they have always deserved but too rarely pursued. LaSonya wrote this book for the faith leader she once was — the one doing extraordinary work without the federal resources to sustain it. Her debut title, Navigating SAM.gov: The Small Business Owner's Complete Registration Guide, opened the door. This book walks you through it.

LaSonya is available for speaking engagements, workshops, and consulting with faith-based organizations, nonprofits, and small businesses navigating the federal contracting landscape.

LaSonya DeBose

pen2paperpublishers.com

www.ingramcontent.com/pod-product-compliance
Lightning Source LLC
LaVergne TN
LVHW010948110826
845149LV00015B/3265

9798995877622